# ABNORMAL PSYCHOLOGY

*An Interactive Cases and Activities Handbook*

**LANI C. FUJITSUBO**
*Southern Oregon University*

Mayfield Publishing Company
Mountain View, California
London • Toronto

*To the clients who have allowed me to share their healing processes, to my students who continually teach me, to my colleagues who inspire and guide me, and to my family and friends who are always there for me.*

Copyright © 2000 by Mayfield Publishing Company

All rights reserved. No portion of this book may be reproduced in any form or by any means without written permission of the publisher.

International Standard Book Number 0-7674-1424-1

Manufactured in the United States of America
10 9 8 7 6 5 4 3 2 1

Cover art: Ewa Gavrielov

Mayfield Publishing Company
1280 Villa Street
Mountain View, California 94041

This book is printed on recycled paper

# CONTENTS

Chapter 1     The Death of Danielle Wood    1

Chapter 2     Paradigms and Perspectives, Models and Methods    7

Chapter 3     Psychological Assessment, Classification, and Clinical Decision Making    13

Chapter 4     The Anxiety Spectrum: From Everyday Worry to Panic    17

         Activity 4-1    25
         Activity 4-2    29
         Activity 4-3    33
         Activity 4-4    35

Chapter 5     Effects of Stress on Health and Disease    37

         Activity 5-1    43
         Activity 5-2    47
         Activity 5-3    49
         Activity 5-4    53
         Activity 5-5    55
         Activity 5-6    59

Chapter 6     The Substance Abuse Disorder Spectrum    63

         Activity 6-1    71

Chapter 7     Dissociative, Somatoform, and Factitious Disorders    75

         Activity 7-1    81
         Activity 7-2    89

Chapter 8     The Mood Disorder Spectrum: From the Blues to Depressive and Bipolar Disorders    93

         Activity 8-1    101
         Activity 8-2    107
         Activity 8-3    109

Chapter 9     The Schizophrenias and Other Psychotic Disorders    113

         Activity 9-1    121
         Activity 9-2    123
         Activity 9-3    125
         Activity 9-4    127
         Activity 9-5    131

**Chapter 10     Personality and Impulse-Control Disorders    135**

        Activity 10-1    143
        Activity 10-2    147
        Activity 10-3    149

**Chapter 11     Intellectual and Cognitive Disorders    151**

        Activity 11-1    157
        Activity 11-2    159
        Activity 11-3    163
        Activity 11-4    169
        Activity 11-5    171

**Chapter 12     Disorders of Childhood and Adolescence    173**

        Activity 12-1    183
        Activity 12-2    191
        Activity 12-3    193
        Activity 12-4    197
        Activity 12-5    199
        Activity 12-6    201

**Chapter 13     Sexual and Related Problems of Adult Life    203**

        Activity 13-1    209
        Activity 13-2    213
        Activity 13-3    217

# PREFACE

Abnormal psychology is one of the most fascinating, exciting, and complex areas within psychology. This cases and activities handbook was written as a tool to help you witness and apply various facets of abnormal psychology. Learning is a dynamic relationship. For learning to occur in the most effective manner, you should be engaged with the material in such a way that you are experiencing and discovering answers and, more important, generating new questions. The case studies and vignettes presented in this book are to be used as learning tools. Remember that no two people are ever the same, and each individual must be viewed within his or her unique circumstances.

This handbook was written to be used in conjunction with *Abnormal Psychology* by Steven Schwartz, and the chapters in this book duplicate the order of the chapters in the textbook. This handbook was designed to provide "real-life" applications of the theories and *DSM-IV* descriptions of mental disorders. The criteria and terminology used in diagnosing the various disorders adheres to the *DSM-IV*. However, because human beings seldom, if ever, fall cleanly within artificial categories, these case studies and vignettes challenge you to view clients as whole and complex people. All of the case studies are based on work done with clients in various settings—from community mental health clinics to in-patient hospital settings to private practice offices to university counseling centers.

The in-depth case studies presented at the beginning of each chapter are designed to help you understand the individuals beneath the diagnostic labels. It is important to remember that clients are not just labels, that they have complex histories and worlds that are touched and affected by what is happening to them emotionally. It is my hope that you will see the clients as courageous, hurt, scared, and complete human beings who are doing the best that they can while needing some support and guidance to overcome whatever is blocking their sense of wholeness and well being.

After you read each case study, turn to one of the activities that has vignettes. These are designed to help you experience sociocultural considerations, ethical concerns, and treatment alternatives. Many of these activities are experiential in nature. I hope you will enjoy these activities and develop an empathetic understanding of what it must be like to experience disorders such as auditory hallucinations or severe memory problems.

This book was designed to address different learning styles and ways of thinking. Some of the questions asked have no right or wrong answers, and some activities were designed to stimulate more questions and theories.

## ACKNOWLEDGMENTS

I would like to especially thank the clients who have shared their pain and hurt with me while allowing me the honor of witnessing them courageously heal and grow. I would like to thank Southern Oregon University for providing me with an amazing place to work and the best colleagues in the world. Thank you to Frank Graham, Mary Johnson, Susan Shook, and Lynn Rabin Bauer at Mayfield Publishing Company for making this book possible. A special thank you to Murl Tucker for sharing his stories and experiences. A very special thank you to the ya-ya's—Ellyn Hersom and Jan Girod—for their continual support, inspiration, sustenance, laughter, and pokes during this process. And finally, a special thank you to the members of my family, who are always there for me.

# CHAPTER 1

# THE DEATH OF DANIELLE WOOD

Jennie is a 20-year-old college sophomore. She is slight of build with long dark hair and large expressive brown eyes. Attending a small liberal arts college in Wisconsin, she is an A student who studies hard and is very disciplined in her work habits. Jennie is quiet and shy, staying mostly to herself. She lives at home with her parents.

Jennie decided to take a dual major in biology and psychology in preparation for medical school. During her first year she took the introductory psychology course. Jennie liked the professor, a female, a lot, but because the class had 75 students and Jennie was very shy, she never spoke to the professor. At the end of her first year, Jennie enrolled in a personal growth and adjustment course given by this professor. It was a class of only 25 students. The course required students to participate in a lot of personal self-exploration and journal writing. Jennie had never done any journal writing or therapy and was rather intimidated by the thought of having to share her innermost thoughts and feelings with anyone else. However, she decided that if she was to be a good doctor one day she had better learn to like herself and to get over her intense shyness.

Jennie struggled with the small-group exercises, feeling extremely uncomfortable and self-conscious. Her thoughts alternated between extreme astonishment at what other people were willing to say out loud to almost complete strangers and feelings of inferiority over not being able to contribute very much. On the first day of class, while in small groups, it was all Jennie could do to give her name and her major. What follows is Jennie's first personal journal entry.

> This feels so strange. I don't think that I can do this. I don't want to look at my feelings or my thoughts. What if they are abnormal or wicked? I hate talking in front of people. I know they will not like me, or think that I am stupid. I don't think that I can do this class. I will go talk to the registrar about dropping this class. Two people in class (I can't remember their names) were very nice to me and tried to get me to feel more a part of the group. Most people in the class were not mean; well, none of them were mean. Most people just ignored me. Most people always just ignore me. Sometimes I feel pretty invisible. The teacher said this journal entry was supposed to be 1–2 pages long. I don't have much else to say. I feel dumb sitting here writing about nothing. It would be so much easier if I could just write a research report. I couldn't believe how much people shared about themselves—telling the whole class (a bunch of strangers!) about their divorces, episodes with drugs and alcohol, problems with children. . . . I would never tell anyone if I had any of those problems. That's all I can think of saying. I hope I won't lose any points for not writing more.

**PERSONAL HISTORY**

Jennie was born in a small rural town adjacent to the city where the college is. Her parents were first-generation immigrants from Yugoslavia. When her parents first immigrated to the United States, they lived in a section of New York City called Little Slovakia. Her father was a tailor and her mother a seamstress. Because neither parent spoke English, they depended on Jennie for the everyday transactions needed to survive. While living in Little Slovakia, Jennie's parents were surrounded by uncles, aunts, and cousins who all spoke the same language, went to the same church, and socialized together. They had little need to talk to or interact with anyone outside their extended families. However, something happened within this small community—Jennie's parents never told her what happened—and there was a split. Jennie's parents and two of her uncles and their families moved to the Midwest. They chose the small town where Jennie was born because it promised employment for her father and her uncles. Also, their church had a strong following in this region.

Jennie was born shortly after her parents relocated. She described her family's adjustment to their new home as very difficult. No one in the small town spoke Slovakian. However, both her uncles and all of her cousins spoke English. Her father got a job working as a tailor. Her mother stayed home to care for Jennie, while also growing a huge garden and selling vegetables and canned fruit for extra income. Jennie remembers both of her parents rising before the sun and working until almost midnight 6 days a week. Jennie's family was very religious. The 1 day a week they did not work was spent in church, and they strictly adhered to all the tenets of their religion. Their social life revolved around their church as well.

Jennie remembered her parents as being serious, dedicated, and somber. Life was to be lived according to very strict rules and guidelines. Jennie herself was very disciplined in all she did—schoolwork, housework, and athletics.

**Journal entry:** Today we talked about families in class. It was very strange and sad. So many of my peers come from dysfunctional homes. Over and over in my small group people shared about coming from alcoholic families, divorced families, or of being abused as children. I was horrified at how casually people spoke of being beaten or of never seeing their fathers. How can this be? The strangest thing of all in class was that after I shared a little about my family several of the people in my group tried to reach out to me in pity—or maybe they were trying to be compassionate. I could not understand why they would feel the need to feel sorry for me. I was very baffled. I think I was the fortunate one. My parents would never divorce. They have never fought in front of me. They have never yelled at me or hit me. I would never think of doing anything disobedient. The other students were laughing about the stunts they pulled when they were younger. I was horrified. I don't know what would have happened to me, but I know I would never have been allowed to disrespect my parents. I really feel like I don't belong in this class. I think I must be very different, because I don't understand most of the time.

Jennie's elementary school, which she called very good, was part of her church. From first to sixth grade she attended a one-room school. She went to school with the same children she went to church with and played with. Until she reached her teens, she can remember talking to people who were not church members only a couple of times a year. The few times she did speak to strangers, it was usually because her parents needed her to translate for them. Jennie did not remember if she was shy when she was a child. She said that children only spoke when spoken to, and she remembered long periods of time when she did not speak at all. She did not remember being afraid of strangers because everyone she came into contact with she knew. The few times she saw strangers, her parents were with her.

The church school only went through the sixth grade, so the following year Jennie attended the public junior high school. Jennie said it was like entering a whole different world. She had no idea what was expected of her. She knew she looked different from all the other students—she wore a simple dress, knee socks, and oxford shoes. She had never cut her thick brown hair and wore it in a long braid down her back. Other girls in her class were wearing short skirts, tank tops, boots, overalls, and shorts. Jennie described being in the classroom as overwhelming. "Everyone was talking at once, people were lounging around their desks, they were listening to radio headsets, chewing gum, and sleeping! When the teacher came in he was dressed in shorts, sandals, and had a ponytail!" She described herself as trying to hide out in a corner. "I didn't want to call attention to myself, but I really wanted to learn."

Jennie made no friends but continued to achieve academically. She felt her academic success was mostly due to the strict education she had received at her church school and the fact that very little seemed to be expected of her in this school. Jennie remembered a time in eighth grade when the class was assigned to do a report on a country. She worked long hours in the library researching her country and put in hundreds of hours on the report. When she finished, it was 50 pages long. Her teacher, overwhelmed, gave her an A++. Jennie also remembered being dumbfounded when she overheard two classmates talking about their reports. One girl wrote her report in two nights, and another hadn't started it until the night before it was due and had to stay up all night to finish it. What discouraged Jennie was that these girls had gotten As on their reports.

**Journal entry:** Sometimes I really feel like a person from another planet. I know most of my school peers think I am strange. Some have even told me that I seem too serious and that I work too hard. One person said that he was always on the lookout for me in classes because he knows if I'm in a class that the curve will be really high. How strange. Sometimes I can't help but think that some of these people actually seem to take great pride in the fact that they put so little work into their schooling. I hear them bragging about how little they study, how they pick the easiest teachers, and how they can "skate" through school. I don't understand. Don't they want to learn? Don't they realize how important all of this is and what an honor it is to be here? When we were sharing in small groups today I told my group that I study 8 to 10 hours a day. They all looked at me like I was crazy. They asked me a lot of questions—like: "Don't you get sick of studying?" "Why do you do it?" "Don't you have a life?" I was pretty confused after class. I had always taken pride in the fact that I worked hard at my studies. Now I can see that others might think I'm abnormal. I wonder if I am abnormal. What does normal feel like? It should be like taking your temperature, 98.6°–normal. . . . What if I am really abnormal? I know I'm not like other people in many ways, but is that wrong? Is being different the same thing as being abnormal? Does this mean that I can never really function outside of my family and church? Now I'm really feeling scared.

When Jennie was in her first year in high school, she still had not made any friends at school. However, one of her teachers, Ms. Hollis, took a special interest in Jennie and made a point to talk to her privately. Ms. Hollis asked Jennie what she wanted to be, what she was interested in, and what sort of things made her happy. Reticent and shy at first, Jennie eventually began to open up to Ms. Hollis. She said that ever since she had read a book about Albert Schweitzer she had wanted to be a doctor. But, she didn't think she'd be able to be a doctor because nobody in her family had ever finished high school, much less attended college. Ms. Hollis encouraged Jennie to explore the possibility of becoming a doctor. Ms. Hollis was also the girls' track coach and asked Jennie to try out for the team. After a great deal of discussion with her parents, Jennie agreed. Much to Ms. Hollis's surprise Jennie turned out to be a naturally gifted long-distance runner who had athletic talent and the perseverance and discipline necessary to train. Jennie enjoyed the training and workouts a lot, and much to her surprise she enjoyed the competition. A much bigger surprise for Jennie was the sense of comradery and belongingness that she experienced for the first time with people outside of her family and church. Jennie excelled in all the tournaments, and by the end of the year she had helped the team qualify for the state championships.

**Journal entry:** Today in class we talked about commitment and personal integrity. I was very surprised how few of my peers seemed to really understand what that meant. It seems as though everyone views life as sort of disposable and negotiable. If you don't like your boyfriend, you break up and find yourself a new one. If you don't like your spouse, you get divorced. If you don't like your job, you quit. This is so strange to me. In my family it seems that we gain integrity by sticking things out. If my father doesn't like his job (which he would never, ever admit to), he gains respect and integrity by making it the best he can. If he has to work 50 hours a week, he does it with pride. He does not feel victimized or taken advantage of. He does it because he must.

I shared a personal story in small group today in class for the first time. I told my peers about the time I had qualified to go to the state championships in track. I had enjoyed being a part of the track team, and I was a good runner. Our team had made it to the state championships for the first time in 10 years that year. I was very happy about it until I found out that the meet would be on Saturday. In my religion Saturday is a holy day. Nobody works on Saturday; we spend the whole day going to church. I told my coach I would not be able to participate in the meet. She was very disappointed. She said without me they would not be able to qualify for the championship. She tried to talk me into running on that day. I could not. She told the team of my decision, and they all seemed to think I was a bad person. I felt terrible that I was making everyone so disappointed. But I had no choice, and no one could understand it. After that experience I was ostracized from the team. It made me sad. But, I would make the same decision again. Several people in my small group thought I was wrong. One girl called me a "drama queen." She said I was "so 'Chariots of Fire.'" I don't know what that means, but judging by her tone I'm sure it is not good. I cannot understand how they could not understand. I feel like I am a whole different species. Some group members commended me on standing by my values. I do not think this is appropriate either—just by their inherent nature values require personal integrity. Am I wrong? Once again I question whether I am abnormal. Is something seriously wrong with me?

After that one attempt at athletics Jennie decided to focus on academics. She excelled in school and after graduating received a scholarship to the local college. This was the only college that Jennie's parents allowed her to apply to. They did not fully support her going to college but were willing to allow her to go provided she continue to live at home and attend church.

Once at college, Jennie began to feel a lot of stress and anxiety. Her high school had not been very large or academically challenging, and she was overwhelmed by the size of the college and felt herself behind many of the other students. Jennie entered college determined to work as hard as she could in order to get top grades, but this was more difficult than Jennie had anticipated. She had always achieved top grades in high school, but now she was competing with other top students who had as much drive as she. Jennie studied 8 to 12 hours a day. All she did was attend classes and study. Pretty soon Jennie was getting only 4 or 5 hours of sleep a night. She was used to working hard, and her parents were not concerned about her long hours of studying, but by the end of her first year Jennie was exhausted. She had lost 20 pounds, had dark circles under her eyes, and rarely smiled. After a summer of working on the farm and studying without the pressure of attending classes, Jennie felt better.

**Journal entry:** Today in class we talked about relaxation, leisure time, and balance. What is all that? It was almost like the class was talking in a foreign language. These are not concepts that have any reality for me. Relaxation and leisure time are wasteful. I have never seen either of my parents just sit and relax. We have never had a television, and any reading was done in order to learn. Life is meant to be lived, and that means to work and achieve. Relaxation, leisure time, and balance seem like nice ways of saying *lazy*. I will admit that I think I worked too hard last year, but far better that than being lazy. Once again I have to wonder how different I am from others. I am really beginning to question my reality. I am feeling a lot of anxiety over being so different. Maybe the things my parents have taught me aren't the only right things. If this is true than I am in *big* trouble, because that means that I have lost my sense of direction and right and wrong. Can normal be relative? I can feel people in class trying hard to relate to me and to include me in their discussions. I'm starting to feel like I'm being sucked away and that there's this big glass wall between me and the rest of the world and that every day that wall is getting thicker and thicker. I've never wanted to touch the others before, and I certainly have never wanted them to touch me, but now that I feel I can't, I feel empty inside. Maybe I am crazy.

During the summer, Jennie saw a doctor because she had stopped menstruating and was not feeling well. The doctor showed a great deal of concern over Jennie's weight loss and run-down appearance. He explained that Jennie's amenorrhea was due to her low body weight and exhaustion and urged her to pace herself and not work herself into this state of exhaustion. Jennie began to cry uncontrollably and tried to explain that she didn't have a choice. The doctor recommended that Jennie seek professional counseling. Jennie reacted like she had been slapped in the face.

**Journal entry:** Today in class we talked about counseling and asking for help when we need it. I was very surprised to find out how many of my peers had been in counseling. And even more surprising was the fact they were not in the least ashamed to admit it. In my family there is a big stigma attached to anyone who cannot handle their own problems. In fact, I remember telling my parents that I wanted to be a doctor and that I thought double majoring in biology and psychology would be excellent preparation for my medical studies. They did not understand what psychology was, and when I tried to describe it for them they thought it was really quite strange. People should handle their own problems, and if they cannot, then family should handle it for them. I asked my parents what would happen if family could not handle it. They said they had never heard of such a thing, but they supposed that the church would then step in to help. Telling a complete stranger your problems would never be an option.

I will confess to you that last summer my doctor recommended that I seek counseling to help me with stress. I was appalled and confused. I knew my parents would never allow me to seek counseling, but a part of me knew I needed help. So, after this class I called the counseling center on campus. It was a very difficult thing to do— my hands were sweating and I felt sick to my stomach. They made an appointment for me for yesterday. Well, I couldn't sleep all night the night before. I was nervous and sick to my stomach. I went in to the counseling center and was so ashamed of being there. A nice woman came out and introduced herself (I was so nervous I can't remember her name now). We went into her office, and she asked why I was there. I started to answer, but told her I had to go because I was going to be sick. I ran to the bathroom and threw up. I don't think I need counseling that badly. I will try to help myself.

1. Is Jennie mentally ill?

2. Would you describe Jennie's behavior as unusual? Why or why not?

3. Would you agree that Jennie's behavior produced distress? Why or why not?

4. Would you consider Jennie's behavior functional? Why or why not?

5. Would you say that Jennie's behavior violated cultural norms? Why or why not?

6. Do you think that Jennie's behavior was caused by an illness? Why or why not?

# CHAPTER 2

# PARADIGMS AND PERSPECTIVES, MODELS AND METHODS

Jason, a 27-year-old White male, was referred to Dr. Kinzie for treatment after being released from the emergency room where he received medical attention for a fall he had taken when drunk. Jason did not want counseling, but a judge had mandated that Jason receive counseling or be fined for trespassing, as he had been partying with friends at an abandoned apartment building. Jason agreed to counseling, but denied he had a problem with alcohol, stating that he could control his drinking and that this was an isolated incident. According to statements the police took from Jason's friends at the time of the incident, however, this was not an isolated incident, but part of a pattern of behavior.

## PERSONAL HISTORY

Jason was born in a small town in rural eastern Oregon to a 19-year-old mother. She was using alcohol and marijuana at the time of conception, but tried to give up both after she discovered she was pregnant. However, she did not know she was pregnant until she was into her second trimester, and, while she was able to abstain from alcohol during the rest of her pregnancy, she continued to use marijuana once or twice a week. Jason's mother was not certain who Jason's father was, but she believed him to be one of two men. Both are still known to Jason and his mother, and both are heavy users of alcohol and marijuana. Jason's mother continued to use both alcohol and marijuana during Jason's childhood.

Jason's mother had left her home when she was 15. Her mother and stepfather were alcoholics, and her stepfather had sexually abused her from the time she was 9 until she left home. Once she left home, she lived on a commune with 25 to 30 adults. Their main source of income was selling marijuana grown on the commune. The members of the commune also made candles and beaded jewelry, which they sold at flea markets and craft festivals. Jason described growing up on the commune as "a continual Deadhead concert—no one ever grew up." Jason spoke with some bitterness about his early life on the commune.

> Nobody knew how to be a parent and do the things parents are supposed to do. There were no real limits. I could come and go as I wanted. No one thought to parent me much. Which was good and bad. It was great to have total freedom to do drugs and stuff, but it was bad because no one took care of me. I never went to the dentist or had to drink milk or eat vegetables. My teeth are a mess because nobody cared about them. [He opened his mouth to show Dr. Kinzie. His teeth were black and brown and they were very small, as though he still had his baby teeth.] My teeth are all rotted out. My mouth hurts a lot most of the time. The dentist that I saw when I was 14 told my foster mother that I would need to have all of them pulled and either have dentures or implants. I was just a kid! My foster mother told the dentist that I was a welfare kid—he pretty much told us that Medicaid would never pay for implants and that I would need dentures. I freaked. I cried and cried and refused to go back to the dentist. I ran away from my foster home in order not to have to go back to the dentist. They found me and placed me in another foster home, and then another and then another, and so on and so on and so on. . . . I was never in another foster home long enough to be taken to the dentist again. And to be honest, no one cared enough to bother fighting with me to make me go.
>
> I remember figuring out how screwed up my life on the commune was when I was around 12. I had sort of been going to school, well, kind of off and on. No one on the commune really cared if I went or not. I used to kind of like going, but it was a problem sometimes in that we lived way the hell out in the boonies. I used to bum rides from some of the guys on the commune if they were going into town, but that didn't happen very often. A truant officer came by when I was 9 or 10. At that time there were only a couple of us young kids living on the commune. He told my mom I had to go to school, it was the law. She promised to make me go—like it was my fault I wasn't going! The truant officer arranged for the school bus to stop and pick a couple of us up and take us to school. School was a total trip. I lived in a pretty small town and there were mostly redneck farmers and timber people. They thought us hippies were from Mars. This was the first time I had really ever spent time with

people who weren't from the commune. It was tough for me. I had a lot of trouble paying attention and following rules—I never had to before. A couple of the people on the commune had taught some of us how to read and write and do math and stuff, so I wasn't too far behind.

I really sort of liked school. I liked the way it was regimented—everyone knew what to expect, and when to expect it. Life at school was predictable. Of course I still had trouble with discipline. I got bored really easily and didn't get along with a lot of the other kids. But by the end of the first year I was more than caught up with the other kids my age and I really liked learning. In fact, to be honest with you, I loved the strokes I would get from the teachers when I did well in school. It was great. Some of the guys at the commune would kind of tease me about how seriously I took learning, but most of them were supportive.

Well, this all lasted for about another year. When I was 12, we had a class on sex education. Now, as I look at it, 12 is way too late to be trying to educate a bunch of kids about sex, but that's how it was done. As we were talking about things, I don't know what happened, but I decided to show off. Usually I just sort of passively sat in the back and minded my own business. Well this time I started bragging about how I had already done all of this stuff—and more besides. It was true, but stupid of me to tell everyone. Well, the teacher was kind of shook up and at lunch asked me to come to the principal's office for a talk. Nothing good ever comes from a talk in the principal's office, I can tell you that! Well, they began asking me if I knew the difference between good touch and bad touch. I never heard of such things. I told them so. They asked me if anyone ever touched me on those places that my bathing suit covers! What a funny way to put it. So, I sat back and said, yeah a lot of people have touched my genitals. They looked upset and wanted to know how they were touched, who touched them, etc. Well, to make a long story short, I was being what is termed molested by two of the guys on the commune. They were in their twenties and thirties and they had been sexually abusing me for years. I'm pretty sure my mom knew about it—after all it was a commune and everybody was pretty open about most things. There was this whole mindset that we need to respect each other's choices and not lay guilt trips on anyone. No one ever threatened me or told me not to tell. Who knows.

Well, I was immediately placed in foster care. It was supposed to be temporary, but it ended up being forever. The people on the commune got into a lot of trouble. The authorities found out that the folks on the commune had been giving us marijuana and stuff. In fact, my mom introduced me to pot when I was 7. We all used to sit around and get stoned. I did this all of my growing-up years. In fact, I still crave pot a lot. When we smoked pot we would all sort of cuddle up together. It was the only time I can remember being hugged and touched that wasn't sexual. I really liked getting stoned with my mom. I remember my mom and her friends always talking about how they would rather die than have to live without pot. Life just wasn't worth it if you had to do it straight. It was like a mantra. I guess it's still my mantra.

I always felt like the odd man out. Like I never really fit in. I did get really lucky in that one of the many social workers I had kind of took a liking to me. She saw that I had some brains and that I liked to learn. She helped me when I was in high school. She got extra tutoring for me, signed me up for all the services they had— you know the "send a poor loser child to camp," Big Brothers, sports teams. She was pretty great. In fact, I still write to her now and again. If it wasn't for her I never would have done anything with my life—not like I have done anything much with it, but I would have been a total waste-out without her. Well, the best thing she did for me was to hook me up with this special foundation. Some rich guy set up this foundation to help poor loser kids like me go to college. The foundation paid for everything! They paid for tuition, room and board, books and even gave me a small allowance to live on while I was going to school. I had to take a full-time load and write up a report every year in order to get all this stuff. If I achieve anything in life, it will be because of these guys.

I feel sort of bad. Here they invested all of this money in me, and I'm sort of pissing it all away by partying. I did graduate with a B.S. in sociology. What was I thinking? What the hell am I supposed to do with a B.S. in sociology? I don't even know how I decided to get this degree. I was cruising along and all of a sudden it was my senior year and I needed to finally declare some sort of major. I had no friggin' idea what to declare. I was just sort of going with the flow. I just took what the catalog told me I had to take, and then I took classes that weren't too early in the morning and that looked kind of interesting. I never had a plan or anything. In desperation I finally sought out some advising. This new faculty guy and I met and stared at my transcript. He asked me what I wanted to be. What a head trip that was. No one had ever asked me that before. I didn't know I even had a choice as to what I wanted to be. I just sort of thought I would be what I am. I was kind of blown away that I had a choice as to what to be. I still can't quite wrap my head around this being thing. It's pretty cool, yet if you really think on it, it's scary as hell. I couldn't answer him, so we just looked at all my classes and decided I should declare sociology as my major because I had the most classes in that—actually it was only one more class than I had in psychology or political science. I didn't know what a sociologist did, I just kind of figured they did social work and that was cool. Well, no big surprise that I was wrong, eh? But, it was cool, I graduated.

The foundation actually offered me the chance to go to graduate school if I wanted to. I kind of freaked and didn't ever get back to them with an answer. Back when I graduated, the last thing I wanted to do was more school. Now that I've been working in construction for a couple of years, I think I may want to go back to school. I like construction okay, but I really do think I want to be a social worker and help out kids like me. First, I guess I'd better get my stuff together, eh?

Dr. Kinzie and Jason worked out a plan for continuing therapy. Jason admitted that he had a problem with alcohol and marijuana and that he wanted to work through some of the things that had happened to him when he was a child. As a teen he had received some counseling concerning the sexual abuse, but he claimed that he wasn't ready to deal with the issues then. He stated that he now realized that his past continues to impact his life. He still fought the mantra that the only way to get through life is stoned because, he said, it was never proven untrue. Jason went through detoxification for alcohol and marijuana and he continued in therapy with Dr. Kinzie.

1. Make an argument that Jason's problems stem from a biogenetic component. Give specific examples from the case study as evidence.

*Jason's problems appear to stem from a biogenetic component as it is clear from his own history and also from his family history that there has been alcohol and drug abuse. His mother was using alcohol and marijuana at the time of conception and continued using it throughout the pregnancy. Jason's family history shows drug abuse and his own recollection of events in his life proves it. Genetics play a role since he has genes from both alcoholic parents.*

2. Assuming that Jason's problems do stem from a biogenetic component, what would your treatment plan be?

*My treatment plan for Jason would be family counseling, and for him to continue with the therapy with Dr Kinzie.*

*- I also suggest Restricted Environmental Stimulation Therapy (REST) which is a psychotherapeutic practice that would place Jason in an environment with a drastically reduced level of external stimulation such as abstinence from alcohol and drug use*

3. Make an argument that Jason's problems arise from a psychodynamic perspective. Give specific examples from the case study as evidence.

From a psychodynamic perspective, abnormal behavior arises from unconscious conflict originating in childhood. Jason's childhood years living in a commune, doing drugs are strong indicators that although he may have wanted to get away from all these, there was no way out. For example, he had no one to take care of him physiologically and when put into foster homes, knowing he wasn't cared for, created an inner conflict within him that made him do drugs and alcohol unconsciously.

4. Assuming that Jason's problems do arise from a psychodynamic conflict, what would your treatment plan be?

Hypnotize him to get his repressed memories back — client centered therapies. (one-on-one)

5. Make an argument that Jason's problems are the result of behavioral reinforcements. Give specific examples from the case study as evidence.

For Jason, doing drugs and stuff seems like he is being rewarded and given the freedom to do whatever he wanted to do. There wasn't any positive reinforcement that would have refrained him from doing it, and he learned this by just observing and unconsciously learning. Jason thought that he can't do anything about it — he had the feeling of "learned helplessness". "His mom introduced him to pot when he was 7."

6. Assuming that Jason's problems are the result of behavioral reinforcements, what would your treatment plan be?

Do therapy to take him off the drugs and alcohol. Reward him when therapy is completed.
- Behavior therapy - observing his behavior and modifying it. Jason would monitor his behavior carefully and keep record. He would establish set of specific goals that will result in gradual behavior change
- Give assignments to Jason and reward him when done.

7. What evidence do you find to support a hypothesis that Jason's problems are humanistic or existential in origin? Give specific examples from the case study as evidence.

Since everyone in the commune did drugs, for Jason this was normal, therefore he didn't know that doing drugs was wrong. He realized this wasn't true when he was around 12 years old. He felt really good about doing pot. It seemed this was the only time he remember being hugged and touched that made him feel good.

8. Assuming that Jason's problems are humanistic or existential in nature, what would your treatment plan be?

Treatment plan -
Ask him to take part in learning workshops and talk to other people who have had similar experiences. Talk to support groups, and be involved with community activities.
- Maybe ask him to take an attitude test to figure out his attitude towards drug and alcoholism.
- or suggest hypnosis.

9. Make an argument that Jason's problems are the result of cognitive thinking errors. Give specific examples from the case study as evidence.

Jason is taking the blame for his behavior. For example he said: "I always felt like the odd man out," and that he never really fitted when sent to foster homes. He also feels bad that the Big Brother foundation has invested money for his education and he was partying instead of studying.

10. Assuming that Jason's problems are cognitive in nature, what would your treatment plan be?

Cognitive Behavior Therapy (CBT) — a combination of therapies by exposing Jason to drugs slowly and increasing it until he says he doesn't want anymore.

11. What sociocultural factors would you need to consider in diagnosing and treating Jason?

I would consider where he lived in his childhood and where he lives now.
Rule out stereotyping — ex. if everyone in the commune did drugs, doesn't mean he has to do it as well.
— Is it normal in his culture to do drugs?
— whether Jason is open minded about getting treatment.

12  CHAPTER 2 / PARADIGMS AND PERSPECTIVES, MODELS AND METHODS

# CHAPTER 3
# PSYCHOLOGICAL ASSESSMENT, CLASSIFICATION, AND CLINICAL DECISION MAKING

Assume that you are a psychologist working in a state mental hospital before the advent of the classification of mental illnesses in the *Diagnostic and Statistical Manual.* You realize it might be highly advantageous to develop such a classification system.

1. List the pros and cons of developing a standardized system of classification for mental illnesses.

    **Pros**                                **Cons**

2. In developing your new system of classification, do you think only the necessary information concerning the mental illness should be included or do you think information concerning the whole person (family, medical needs, and so on) should be included? Or should the classification be something in between the two? Explain your decision.

3. Based on your answer to question 2, develop a system of classification for mental illness.

4. A 53-year-old divorced White woman has come to you for therapy. She said that since her divorce 6 months ago she has been crying all the time, feeling really sad and angry, not eating, and sleeping all the time. She has missed so much work that she fears that her boss may fire her. Having lost all interest in her hobbies and friends, she has become desperate. Using the model you developed for question 3, diagnose this woman.

5. What were the strengths and weaknesses of your new classification system?

6. After completing your classification, what further information would help you make a better diagnosis?

7. If you were to refer this client to a colleague in another city, how helpful would your diagnostic classification be to your colleague?

8. How might you assess the reliability and validity of your new classification system?

# CHAPTER 4

# THE ANXIETY SPECTRUM: FROM EVERYDAY WORRY TO PANIC

Maria is a 28-year-old White female who called for therapy complaining of feeling a great deal of fear, anxiety, and apprehension. She and her husband, an army doctor, had recently relocated to Fairbanks, Alaska. Maria stated that she was so frightened to stay at home when no one was there that she had to leave the house when her husband left. She spent the day driving around or just sitting in her car waiting until her husband returned home. This was becoming extremely problematic because winter, with sub-zero temperatures, was approaching. Maria described her days as a "wash of worry and anxiety."

Maria was a beautiful, petite woman, with an olive complexion, large dark eyes, and long black hair. She carried herself with a dancer's grace and dressed in expensive, tasteful clothes. While she always looked perfectly groomed and attired, she seemed unaware of her appearance. There are several mirrors in the office, which Maria never looked at. She never fussed with her clothing, hair, or makeup. While she described being highly anxious and worried, she sat still, made appropriate eye contact, and only occasionally displayed the slightest sign of anxiety by playing with the tea bag in her teacup.

**PERSONAL HISTORY**

Maria was one of two children, older than her brother by 2 years. She described her family as very close. Her parents were second-generation Italians, and she grew up in the Italian section of a large East Coast city. Her father worked hard and built a successful music store; the family lived in an apartment above the store. Her mother helped in the store but spent most of her time cleaning and cooking. The apartment was always immaculate, and the family ate every meal together. Maria describes every breakfast, lunch, and dinner as a feast. If Maria ever said she wanted something special for a meal, her parents would "break their necks" getting and preparing it. As a result, she learned early not to ask for anything. However, there was always a lot of pressure to say what she wanted. When talking about this family dynamic, Maria laughed, stating, "It became a kind of game. My parents would make the first move by hinting and asking what I wanted, then I would have to try to figure out what it was that was already planned, or what *they* really wanted so that I could say the right thing. I think the score was about 50-50."

Maria said that love in her family meant meeting everyone else's needs, no matter the sacrifice to yourself. "I was trained early not to think about my needs. All I knew was that I was supposed to know—although, I'm still not clear as to what I was supposed to know." Maria talked about how strange it felt to try and put all these rules into words and share them with her therapist. She said that everyone was supposed to know the rules, although she can never remember anyone ever actually teaching her or talking about the rules. Maria remembered her mother, father, grandparents, and aunts once discussing the husband of one of her aunts, who didn't follow the rules. This discussion was one of the few times Maria heard anyone in the family speak badly about another family member. From this discussion, Maria—at age 7—learned how awful it was not to know or follow the rules.

Maria went to Catholic school until high school. During her childhood, she did not have any friends. "I don't ever remember being lonely because I always had my parents and brother." She was expected to spend her free time helping her mother cook and clean, playing with her brother, visiting relatives, going to church, and doing homework. "I guess it sounds pretty weird now, but I remember having a really happy childhood." Maria described herself as a happy, serious, good little girl.

Further into therapy Maria described a bedtime ritual, which seemed to surprise and embarrass her. Maria stated that she hadn't remembered this ritual in years. After one of her parents read her a story, she would go to bed and say her prayers, which she described as like a repetitive chant—she always said the same things in the same order—"God bless Mother, Father, Joey, Grandma," and so on, naming all her relatives, teachers, and acquaintances. After her parents kissed her goodnight, Maria would lie in bed on her back, crossing her arms over her chest. She took the same position every night. "I believed that if I could assume the exact right position, I could protect everyone from harm that night. Sometimes it got pretty uncomfortable, but I would sustain that position until I fell asleep." She wasn't sure but thought she might have done this ritual for several years, from age 4 to 8.

Maria never had a special friend or a pet as a child. When asked about favorite books, colors, foods, or clothes, she could not remember ever having had a favorite anything. As she discussed this, she thought it might be a bit odd. Even as an adult, however, Maria rarely if ever developed strong preferences for anything. As she explored this concept, she realized that she is hesitant to develop strong preferences out of fear that her husband or family might not share her preferences—and, she said, "then what?" Everyone in her family enjoyed the same things—from food, to television shows, to books, to music. Maria thought this was a normal phenomenon, true in most American families.

1. What are your initial thoughts about Maria?

2. Do you believe that most American families share the same preferences? Give evidence to support your position.

3. List the preferences you share with other members of your family. Then list the differences you have with one another.

4. Now compare your list with that of a classmate. Did you find similarities? Differences?

5. What might the similarities and the differences mean?

6. How do you think the cultural differences regarding the value placed on individualism and collectivism might affect the responses of different individuals to this exercise?

7. If Maria performed this exercise, what insights do you think she might develop by comparing her list to yours?

8. How might you use this information as a therapeutic tool?

Maria stated that she tried her best to be perfect. Perfection was expected in her family—though no one ever put pressure on her or her brother, it was just one of those rules. Her parents set the example of perfection. Maria describes her home as always being perfectly clean, neat, and organized. Her mother was able to work at the store, maintain a perfect house, take care of Maria and her brother, and cook three gourmet meals every day. Maria stated that both of her parents were in good health and attractive. While food was a big priority in their family, no one ever had any kind of eating disorder. "I have one aunt who is somewhat overweight—10 or 15 pounds. But no one ever talks about it."

Maria made light of her appearance—"I guess I'm OK looking." She stated that she really does not put very much thought into her appearance. Her husband constantly said she was beautiful, but she thought him biased. Maria explained her clothes and grooming as part of the way she was raised. "It is important to make the most of what you have, but to never, ever be vain or conceited about anything." She believed herself "exceedingly average" in her appearance, intelligence, talents, abilities—everything. She remembered her parents being extremely distressed by a small chicken pox scar she has by her left eyebrow. "I remember them apologizing and apologizing for allowing that scar to be there. I remember thinking it looked kind of neat, and now that I am older I think it adds character to my face. I never could understand what my parents were so upset about."

Maria stated that she was pretty much always a good girl. It wasn't until her senior year of high school that she "rebelled." Maria had never dated until that year. The only boys she knew were cousins or their friends. Maria described herself as shy and scared of people outside her extended family. While working part-time in her father's music store, she met Randy, who came into the store to buy sheet music and records. He was 2 years older than Maria and was already attending college, studying to become a doctor. Maria enjoyed talking to him about music and studying. He asked her out on a date, and Maria said yes. When she told her parents, they were extremely upset. Her mother cried, and her father became quiet and sad. Maria had broken a major rule by wanting to date Randy—he was not Italian; her parents did not know his family; and, worst of all, he was Jewish.

Maria and Randy fell in love. They snuck around to see each other because Maria did not want to make her parents sad or upset. After Maria graduated from high school, she decided to go away to college—a big decision for her. Her parents had hoped that she would attend a university in the city and continue to live at home, and Maria had planned on doing just that until she started dating Randy. She and Randy decided that Maria would attend a university in the city where he went to medical school so they could see each other without needing to sneak around. Maria had an interesting insight while discussing this time in her life. She said that she found it interesting that during this time of sneaking around she should have been really anxious, fearful, guilt-ridden, and nervous, but she had never felt freer or happier.

While at the university, Maria drove home every Friday afternoon and returned to the city after eating Sunday dinner with her family. After 2 months, she and Randy moved in together. She had a separate phone line installed just for calls from her parents, who called every day. For 4 years, she continued going home on weekends and holidays, never mentioning Randy to her family. During this time Maria never worked, as her parents financially supported her. At times she felt some guilt about taking their money in order to live with Randy, but she described those years as good overall.

After Maria graduated, she and Randy decided to get married. Randy had received student loans from the army in order to pay for medical school. He now had to spend 4 years working as an army doctor to repay the loans. Randy received orders that he was going to be stationed in San Francisco for at least a year. When Maria told her parents that she was going to marry Randy, "They did not take the news well, no big surprise there. But they did insist that we have a big, and I mean *big*, Catholic wedding. It was the last thing I wanted, but it was the least I could do; after all, I totally screwed them." Immediately after the wedding, Maria and Randy moved to San Francisco.

Maria described the 2 years they spent in San Francisco as wonderful. She did not have to work because Randy's salary was generous. She took art and literature classes, learned gourmet cooking, and spent a lot of time reading. She also made her first friend, Tina, the wife of another physician working on base. Maria described Tina as "liberated, smart, funny, demanding, scary, without any guilt!" This was the first person besides Randy that Maria had ever confided in. While Randy was always a good listener, he never said anything negative about her family. Tina was kind and compassionate but told Maria that her relationship with her family was not normal. Maria began to look at her family differently and started to see that everything might not be perfect. It was then that her anxiety symptoms began. Maria began having trouble sleeping and became fearful of being alone. At the time, she and her parents still spoke daily, and she flew back to visit them once every 6 weeks.

After 2 years in San Francisco, Randy was transferred to Fairbanks, Alaska. It was very difficult for Maria to make this move. She had loved living in San Francisco. She had always lived in a city. She would miss Tina. But Randy had always wanted to live in the country, to fish, hike, and camp, and Maria was willing to give this new lifestyle a chance. She and Randy flew up to Fairbanks and bought a beautiful home in the hills. Maria loved the lushness of the wilderness surrounding Fairbanks. Maria's parents were devastated when Maria told them about the move; they began crying. While they were never critical, her mother said it felt like she was losing Maria all over again. Maria's guilt and doubts returned full-force.

From the beginning of their stay in Fairbanks, Maria was highly anxious. She didn't want to be left alone. She accompanied Randy to work and just sat in an office until he was ready to go home. After a few weeks Randy told her she could no longer do that because of base regulations. After that, she only went with Randy when he was called to the hospital in the middle of the night; then she would sit in the car until he was ready to go home. In the mornings she got in her car when Randy left for work and drove around town all day, or sat in the car, or shopped. She was too nervous to sign up for classes at the university and too unhappy to do volunteer work. She complained of insomnia; rapid heart rate; hyperventilating; sweaty, cold hands; lack of appetite; hypervigilance; being easily scared and startled; trembling in her hands and legs; headaches; and stomach cramps. When she was given a complete physical, the examination showed no physical reasons for her symptoms.

1. Using the *DSM-IV* five-axis model, develop a preliminary diagnosis for Maria.

    Axis I:

    Axis II:

    Axis III:

    Axis IV:

    Axis V:

2. Would your diagnosis be different if, in addition to her other symptoms, Maria complained of hopelessness, helplessness, overwhelming sadness, and loss of joy in everything, lasting for 3 weeks?

3. Would your diagnosis be different if, along with the other symptoms, Maria described a fear of being alone in the house, but she was able to be alone in someone else's home, at a motel, or anywhere but home?

4. Would your diagnosis be different in the following situation: if Maria had fallen off of a ladder at home, knocked herself unconscious and suffered from 3 days of temporary partial paralysis, her symptoms did not begin until she returned home from the hospital, and they were accompanied by a recurring dream that she falls and becomes permanently paralyzed?

Although Maria was extremely anxious and fearful about taking any kind of medication, she agreed to begin taking Zoloft, an antidepressant, and Xanax, a mild antianxiolytic. Both medications have mild side effects, and Maria was started on the lowest dose possible. Maria was placed on these medications because she needed some relief from her anxiety in order to fully participate in any form of psychotherapy. Maria was also beginning to feel desperate for help because winter was quickly approaching.

Maria was treated with cognitive-behavioral therapy. Because Maria was highly motivated and intelligent, she began bibliotherapy using Aaron Beck's and David Burns's books to explain cognitive therapy. Maria was guided to understanding her problems in connection with her thoughts, moods, behaviors, physical reactions, and environment. She was then able to understand how all these areas are interconnected, each affecting every other one.

5. Using this model, how might Maria have responded to each category:

   a. Her thoughts (remember that thoughts are images, memories, and beliefs, not feelings)

   b. Her moods (these are feelings)

   c. Her physical reactions

   d. Her behaviors

   e. Her environment

**Please do not read any further until you have completed the preceding exercise.**

These are among the responses Maria actually gave:

**Thoughts:** "I am a bad person for disappointing my parents." "I will be punished for being a bad person." "Something terrible will happen to someone I love because of me." "If I can be perfect everyone will be safe." "Randy is getting sick of me being so neurotic all the time."

**Moods:** fearful, anxious, sad, lonely, guilty, nervous, ashamed, panicky, embarrassed, depressed.

**Physical reactions:** Insomnia, weight loss, rapid heart rate, shallow breathing, cold, clammy hands, headaches.

**Behaviors:** Avoidance of fear of being alone by driving around and sitting in her car. Dependence on Randy to protect her from her fears.

**Environmental changes:** The move to Fairbanks. A new home. Living in a rural environment as opposed to living in a city. Loss of Tina's friendship. Moving farther away from her family of origin. Having nothing to do all day.

After Maria identified and ranked her feelings, identified situations that caused an increase in negative emotions, and recognized her cognitive distortions, she began to use thought records to challenge her distortions and to develop more balanced thoughts, which positively affected her emotions. When going over the list of cognitive distortions Maria started to laugh. Stating that she did every one of them, she said, "you mean to tell me these are wrong?"

Maria also began doing small behavioral experiments, a type of gradual exposure. She experimented with staying inside the house while Randy was outside. When she could do this with little anxiety, she practiced staying at home for short periods of time while Randy went to the store or gym. Soon Maria was able to stay home alone. She developed some rituals to help her feel safe—she would carry her cellular phone with her from room to room and check all the doors and windows only once after Randy left. In the beginning she was unable to have the stereo or television on while home alone because she felt she needed to be able to hear any possible sound. Being home alone during the day began to cause little anxiety for Maria, but she still had problems when Randy was called out during the night. During these times Maria would get dressed, turn on all the lights, and wait for Randy to return. While these were still rather stressful times, Maria was able to read or knit while waiting for Randy.

Soon after Maria was able to successfully stay home alone, she asked for help on her perfectionism. Along with completing thought records associated with cognitive distortions related to the need to be perfect, Maria agreed to try some behavioral experiments. She stated that she was unable to enjoy hobbies and crafts because she could not do them perfectly right from the start. She spent some time deciding on what things she really wanted to try to learn. She chose playing the guitar, drawing, and knitting. Her first assignment was to spend 30 minutes drawing a picture of anything she wanted. After 30 minutes, she was to tear up the picture and throw it away—even if she really liked what she had drawn. This exercise was designed to give her permission to take chances, make mistakes, and realize that the world would not stop if she was not perfect. Maria completed a series of experiments and exercises, gradually becoming happier and more spontaneous. After several months Maria was able to be home alone and feel secure and happy. She continued in therapy to work through some of the enmeshment issues related to her family and to continue to grow as an individual.

Name _Neeta Narayan_ Section _____ Date _4/16/02_

## ACTIVITY 4-1

**Directions:** Read the following vignettes and answer the questions that follow.

**Vignette 1**

Carol, a 46-year-old female, recently went to the emergency room with what she was sure was a heart attack. She was in the movie theater with her husband and another couple. She had been having an enjoyable evening. While watching the movie, Carol suddenly felt her heart start pounding and beating very fast, she became light-headed and dizzy, she began sweating and trembling, and she realized that her fingers and toes were tingling and numb. Carol was sure she was having a heart attack. She sat there for a few minutes trying to decide what to do. She visualized herself dying in the theater, with paramedics showing up and all the other patrons staring at her. While thinking this, she grew more and more upset. Soon she told her husband that she had to leave and asked him to take her to the hospital. At the hospital Carol was given tests and examined. No evidence of a heart problem was detected, and no physical reasons were found for her symptoms. Carol went home confused and embarrassed, but also relieved. Two weeks later, in the grocery store, Carol had the same symptoms. She quickly left her cart and drove home, but after about 15 minutes, the symptoms abated. Carol became afraid to leave her home. She would not go alone anywhere farther than 10 minutes from her house and would not go longer distances without her husband.

1. What *DSM-IV* diagnosis would you assign to Carol?

    *Axis I - Panic Disorder*

2. What are other possible diagnoses?

    *Agoraphobia*

3. On what criteria do you base your diagnosis?

CHAPTER 4 / THE ANXIETY SPECTRUM: FROM EVERYDAY WORRY TO PANIC     25

**Vignette 2**

Gordon, a 41-year-old male, recently received a prestigious and lucrative promotion, but the new position would require him to do an extensive amount of traveling, and Gordon has a deathly fear of riding in airplanes. The last time he flew, his reactions verged on a full-blown panic attack, with chest pains, nausea, shortness of breath, and the feeling that he was going to jump out of his skin. The flight was only an hour long, but Gordon felt sure he would never make it—he was sure the plane would crash. Gordon realizes that his fears are irrational, but because of this fear of flying he is thinking of resigning his new position.

4. What *DSM-IV* diagnosis would you assign to Gordon?

   *Specific phobia — Phobia of flying*
   *— aerophobia*

5. What are other possible diagnoses?

   *Anxiety disorder*
   *Panic disorder*

6. On what criteria do you base your diagnosis?

**Vignette 3**

Heather, a 19-year-old college junior, has an intense fear of speaking to people she does not know very well. During her first and second years, she chose large lecture courses, which allowed her to hide in the back of the lecture hall and not speak to other students or to participate in class discussions. Heather received high marks in all of her courses, earning a place on the dean's list and the honor roll. In her third year, Heather is now required to take some smaller upper-division courses in which class participation and small-group discussions are mandatory. She is sure that others will judge her or that she will say something foolish. Because of these fears, Heather has had trouble sleeping at night, is not eating, and is considering dropping out of school.

7. What *DSM-IV* diagnosis would you assign to Heather?

    *Social phobia*

8. What are other possible diagnoses?

    *Specific phobia of large groups*

9. On what criteria do you base your diagnosis?

**Vignette 4**

Lauren, a 32-year-old female, was referred for counseling by her medical doctor. Lauren reported feeling "always unhappy and anxious about everything." She was recently fired from her job as a nurse in a large family practice because she was reporting for work later and later and spending more and more time in the ladies room washing her hands. Lauren has a devastating fear of germs and dirt. She understands that her fear is at times irrational, but then she describes the many diseases she has researched—she spends hours each evening on the Internet researching medical journals and has hundreds of notebooks filled with information on diseases. Every one of the thousands of pages in Lauren's notebooks is enclosed in a plastic sleeve. She wears gloves when she works on her notebooks and will not let anyone else touch them. Because Lauren spends so many hours researching these diseases, she only sleeps 3 or 4 hours each night. As a result, she has trouble getting up in the morning. In addition, Lauren has an elaborate ritual for getting ready to leave the house. She has to wipe down all of her notebooks and computer equipment with an antibacterial cleaner. She then has to shower again to clean herself of any possible contamination. She then cleans all the doorknobs and counter surfaces with an antibacterial cleaner. When she arrives at work, she goes through an elaborate cleansing ritual every time she comes into contact with anyone she suspects may have any kind of a disease. Because she works in a doctor's office, she has contact with many, many ill people. Lauren's hands are chapped and raw from all the washing and cleaning she does. Though unhappy, Lauren feels incapable of changing anything.

10. What *DSM-IV* diagnosis would you assign to Lauren?

    *Obsessive Compulsive Disorder*

    *Generalized Anxiety order develops into OCD*

11. What are other possible diagnoses?

    *Specific phobia — mysophobia*
    *nosophobia*

12. On what criteria do you base your diagnosis?

Name _____ Section _____ Date _____

## ACTIVITY 4-2

**Directions**: Listed below are some ways thoughts can be distorted. Distorted thoughts can affect moods. After each definition of a thought distortion, there is an example of an incident. After the incident write out a distorted thought about the incident, then the feelings you might have if you believed that thought. Then write out a rational, nondistorted way of thinking about the same incident and the feelings you might have if you believed this thought. Two examples follow:

**Example 1**

**Overgeneralization: You come to a general (usually negative) conclusion based on a single incident or piece of evidence.**

**Incident:** Last week you finally got the nerve up to ask for a date with someone you have been interested in for a long time. The person said nicely that he or she is already involved with someone else and couldn't go out with you.

**Distorted/irrational thought:** "I'm such a loser. They must think I'm a total jerk. No one will ever want to go out with me."

**Feelings:** Humiliated, inferior, rejected, unlovable.

**More nondistorted/rational thought:** "This person was already involved with someone else and treated me nicely. I'm sure there are other nice people out there who are not already attached. I just need to keep looking."

**Feelings:** Disappointed, regretful, hopeful for the future.

**Example 2**

**Polarized thinking: Everything is either all good or all bad, black or white. There is no middle ground.**

**Incident:** You took your midterm in abnormal psychology and received a C.

**Distorted/irrational thought:** "I'm so stupid. I'm just not college material. I'm such a failure. I can't do this."

**Feelings:** Inadequate, powerless, fearful, defeated, desperate.

**More nondistorted/rational thought:** "The exam was harder than I expected. A C isn't a grade I'm very proud of, but it isn't the end of the world, either. I can still get an A in the class if I do well on the remaining exams. I will just have to study harder for the final. I know I didn't study for this exam as much as I wanted to. I'll make it a priority to study for the next exam."

**Feelings:** Disappointed, determined.

### Situation 1

**Mind reading:** Without people directly telling you anything, you know how they feel about you, what they are thinking, and why they are acting as they do.

**Incident:** You are having lunch in the cafeteria, and your friend Jenny walks right by your table to sit with some other people.

**Distorted/irrational thought:**




**Feelings:**




**More nondistorted/rational thought:**




**Feelings:**




### Situation 2

**Catastrophizing:** Expecting the worst. Waiting for disaster.

**Incident:** You get a headache.

**Distorted/irrational thought:**




**Feelings:**

**More nondistorted/rational thought:**

**Feelings:**

**Situation 3**

**Shoulds, musts, and oughts: You have very specific rules about how you and everyone else should behave.**

**Incident:** You planned a party and invited 12 to 15 friends. You went out of your way to accommodate one friend's schedule. She did not ask you to change anything, but you really wanted to have her come to your party. Two days before the party, she called to tell you that work requires her to travel and she can't come to your party.

**Distorted/irrational thought:**

**Feelings:**

**More nondistorted/rational thought:**

**Feelings:**

**Situation 4**

**Personalization: You believe that everything people do or say is about you. You constantly compare yourself to others—who's better looking, who makes more money, who's more successful, and so on.**

**Incident:** You are at a party and have met someone you really like. This person is funny, attractive, and engaging. After the two of you spend 20 minutes talking and laughing, this person excuses himself to go to the restroom. Five minutes later you see him laughing and talking with a couple of other people.

**Distorted/irrational thought:**

**Feelings:**

**More nondistorted/rational thought:**

**Feelings:**

Name _____ Section _____ Date _____

## ACTIVITY 4-3

Joseph Wolpe believed that a person could not be anxious and relaxed at the same time. Systematic desensitization is based on this premise. Systematic desensitization works well in helping to cure simple phobias. A first step in systematic desensitization is to develop a Subjective Units of Distress (SUD) Scale, which ranks phobic-related stimuli in order of anxiety arousal from least to most. The following exercise, aimed at developing an SUD, can be done individually, in pairs or small groups, or as a class.

One person should volunteer to develop an SUD scale. It works best if that person has a real phobia, but if no one wishes to volunteer to share a phobia, the pair, small group, or class can pick a phobia to work with.

Start by imagining a ranking of 0 to 100 with 0 being no anxiety at all and 100 being high anxiety. Start listing various stimuli related to the object of the phobia and give a number to the degree of anxiety that would be aroused by each stimulus. For example, if someone has a phobia of snakes, the SUD scale might look something like this:

    10 = A picture of a snake in a magazine
    27 = Someone talking about a pet snake in a cage
    38 = Seeing a snake on TV
    49 = Watching someone handle a snake on TV
    68 = Hearing a story about coming on a snake unexpectedly on a walk or in the garden
    75 = Knowing there is a snake in a cage in the next room
    89 = Bringing the caged snake into the room
   100 = Letting the snake out in the room

Now, using a phobia of your own, work out your SUD scale.

The SUD scale is developed to be used in conjunction with relaxation techniques. A person is trained to get into a state of relaxation. Then the therapist asks the person to imagine the lowest-rated scene from his or her SUD scale. The person will then become anxious and will need to work on becoming relaxed again. When the person has successfully been able to relax while imagining that scene, he or she is asked to imagine the next lowest anxiety-arousing scene. Therapy proceeds until the person can remain relaxed while imagining the highest anxiety-arousing scene. Successfully achieving this should lower the anxiety surrounding the person's phobia.

Students might like to try pairing the SUD scale and deep relaxation once or twice to experience this therapy. Students should understand that it usually takes several sessions before clients can become successful with this technique.

**ACTIVITY 4-3** *(continued)*

Name _____ Section _____ Date _____

# ACTIVITY 4-4

This exercise works best if the instructor can guide the entire class through the relaxation at the same time, but it can be done in pairs or even alone.

Create a comfortable and relaxed setting by dimming the lights, playing some soft relaxing music, and having the person who is going to relax get into a comfortable position (either lying down, sitting on the floor, or resting in a chair with both feet on the floor).

In a slow, calm, and melodic voice, read the following aloud to the person who is going to do the relaxation. Do not stare at or watch the person who is relaxing too intently, as this will cause him or her to become self-conscious.

> Get into a comfortable position. If you are sitting in a chair, uncross your arms and legs.
> Close your eyes when you feel ready.
> Slowly take a deep breath. Try to breathe in through your nose, allowing your breath to travel into your lungs. Feel your chest expand, and, when the air reaches deep into your diaphragm, feel your stomach expand.
> As you exhale, feel your breath travel up through your lungs and slowly out of your mouth.
> Take another deep, relaxing breath in through your nose, down into your lungs, into your diaphragm, and out your mouth.
> You may feel some tingling in your chest, hands, arms, and legs. This is normal. Continue to take a few more deep, relaxing breaths. [Wait for the person to complete three or four more breaths.]
> Just by taking these deep, relaxing breaths, your body should start to feel relaxed and heavier.
> Continue to breathe deeply. On your next breath, picture a ball of white light resting on the middle of your forehead. When you breathe in, picture that ball of white light entering your head and traveling down your neck, into your lungs, into your arms, down your torso, into your legs, and out your feet. [Allow the person a couple of minutes to try this.]
> See if you can continue to cycle the ball of white light throughout your body as you continue to breathe deeply.
> As this ball of white light travels through your body, imagine it touching the parts of your body that are tense or hurting and taking away the tension and pain. [Allow the person a couple of minutes to continue circulating the white light.]
> Now, I am going to ask you to tighten, hold, and then release certain muscle groups. We are going to begin with the muscles in your face and head. I want you to scrunch up all your facial muscles and the muscles in your scalp and hold them for the count of three. Ready. 1, 2, 3. [Count slowly.] And release.
> All of those muscles should feel very relaxed now. [Depending on how much time remains, you can ask the students to repeat each group of muscles, or you can continue on to the next group of muscles.] Next, we are going to tighten and hold the muscles in your neck and shoulders. I want

you to pull your shoulders as high up and close to your ears as you can and hold for the count of three. Ready. 1, 2, 3. [Count slowly.] And release.

Good. You should feel more relaxed now.

Now we are going to tighten and hold the muscles in your arms and hands. I want you to make fists with your hands and tighten all your arm muscles, holding for the count of three. Ready. 1, 2, 3. [Count slowly.] And release.

Now, tighten and hold the muscles in your stomach area. I want you to tighten and contract all of your abdominal muscles and hold for the count of three. Ready. 1, 2, 3. [Count slowly.] And release.

Good. Remember to keep breathing deeply. Now tighten and hold your glut muscles. Ready. 1, 2, 3. [Count slowly.] And release.

Excellent. Your body should be feeling more and more relaxed now. The last group of muscles we are going to tighten and hold are your leg and feet muscles. Contract your leg muscles and curl and tighten your feet. Ready. 1, 2, 3. [Count slowly.] And release.

Very good. Your body should feel heavy and relaxed. I want you to breathe in the ball of white light one more time. This time I want you to have that ball of white light touch any place in your body where there still might be some tension or tightness.

Good. Now I am going to ask you to take a deep breath and tell yourself that when you open your eyes, you will continue to feel focused, relaxed, healthy, and energized.

Open your eyes on the count of three. 1, 2, 3. [Remember to count slowly.]

# CHAPTER 5

# EFFECTS OF STRESS ON HEALTH AND DISEASE

Sharon is a 37-year-old White female who has had a recurrence of breast cancer. Sharon refused to undergo chemotherapy or radiation, choosing instead to pursue alternative herbal treatments with a doctor in Mexico. Sharon's first bout with breast cancer happened 5 years before. At that time Sharon tried all the traditional medical treatments and had a mastectomy of her right breast. She had been cancer-free for 5 years.

## PERSONAL HISTORY

Sharon is a divorced mother of four children aged 16, 14, 12, and 9. Sharon had been divorced for a year and a half. Her marriage to Tony had been turbulent and at times semiviolent. Sharon would hit Tony, break his things, and rip his clothes. Tony would forcibly restrain Sharon when she became violent, sometimes sitting on her or bruising her wrists and arms when he was restraining her. After the divorce, Sharon and Tony remained connected to each other and even lived together at times. They both had a strong commitment to their children and tried their best to work together to raise them.

Sharon and Tony were married when they were both 21 years old. They met at college and fell in love. Neither had ever been in a serious relationship before, and both later confessed that they married each other partly because they were afraid that they would never find anyone else. Their marriage was turbulent from the beginning. They were both strongly influenced by their families, and the fact that neither family was very supportive of the marriage caused strife from the beginning.

Tony came from a closed, tight family. His father was a prominent judge, and his mother was a society matron. While both parents were actively involved in the community, they spent very little time with Tony or his younger sister. Tony grew up isolated and unsure of himself. His parents discouraged both Tony and his sister from making friends outside of the family. Tony never learned how to initiate a conversation or make small talk. Tony described himself as a good and nice person who just doesn't know how to relate to other people. While in high school he excelled as a wrestler and runner. His parents never came to see him compete, and the only comments he received from them were critical. Because of the criticism and lack of support, Tony decided not to continue participating in sports in college. In college Tony was an above-average student who faded into the background. As an adult Tony remained very unsure of himself socially and chose to remain apart from people. Tony was attracted to Sharon's ability to see the positive in most situations and to be enthusiastic and encouraging of Tony and others. Sharon had a natural ability to connect with people, which balanced Tony's lack of social skills.

Sharon grew up in a large outgoing family. Her mother was an artist, and her father was a professional writer and artist. She was the fifth child of seven. Initially Sharon presented her childhood as a "wonderful fairy tale" where everybody was encouraged to be creative and pursue their dreams. They never had a television; all the children were too busy writing, drawing, or exploring to sit and watch television. All of the children were well behaved and excelled in school and sports. Later in therapy, however, a darker side emerged. Sharon's mother had difficulty expressing her anger. Her mother went from being loving and caring to being rageful and angry. Sharon described all the children walking on eggshells, never really knowing when their mother would blow up. Sharon reported that she was often the target of her mother's rage. While she was never beaten severely (nothing was ever broken), her mother did slap, hit, and verbally abuse her. While describing her mother, Sharon's body became rigid and her voice and mannerisms precise. She did not raise her voice, but the tone and inflection became tense and hard. Sharon did not cry or express anger, but at times she seemed to be trying to control her tears. When this was pointed out, she stated that she was not aware of any negative feelings toward her mother. She stated that she knows her mother was doing the best she could and that whatever happened in her childhood is over with now and forgiven.

Sharon described her father as gentle and passive. He inspired her to go to college and become excellent at whatever she chose to do in life. He loved the arts and nature and could spend hours painting a flower or reading the same poem over and over. He never raised his voice and would never dream of hitting any of his children. Sharon got teary-eyed when talking about her father. Her voice softened, and her gestures became gentle. She sadly shook her head and cried. When asked about her tears, Sharon stated that she just loved her parents so much. After a few sessions it became clear that while Sharon's father was a source of inspiration and support, he did nothing to protect the children from the abuse. Sharon remembered once begging her father to help her after being beaten by her mother. He just looked at her and cried. After that, Sharon never sought his protection or support.

Sharon wanted to be a teacher. When her children were small, she decided to go back to graduate school. She cared for the children during the day and left when Tony came home from work. Tony cared for them in the evenings and on weekends. He cooked dinner, gave them baths, did their homework with them, and put them to bed. While Tony enjoyed spending time with the children, he resented the workload. Sharon excelled in school and eventually completed two different master's degrees and an elementary education teaching certificate. The master's programs took 6 years to complete and cost thousands of dollars. Tony had supported her in the beginning but grew resentful after the first couple of years.

After completing her education Sharon decided to home-school the children. Tony was supportive of the idea but worried about finances. Tony was an engineer with a medium-sized company. He started working for this company right out of college and was content to stay there until he retired. Tony was not challenged by his job, but he knew he could do it well and it was a good place to work. Tony's parents had always criticized him for his lack of motivation. Insecure about his abilities, Tony felt lucky to have this job. If Tony could pick a slogan to live his life by it would be, "Don't make waves." Tony had never asked for a raise. He was never absent or late for work. He was reliable but didn't shine.

Because Tony had never asked for a raise or a promotion, and with four children and Sharon not working, finances had always been tight and the family had to live on a fairly strict budget. When Sharon decided not to work but to home-school the children Tony became agitated about money. Sharon had large student loan payments. Tony would not tell Sharon how he was feeling, but expressed his anger with passive-aggressiveness. Sharon became hurt and confused. After weeks or months of Tony's passive-aggressive behavior, Sharon would lash out violently. This cycle continued for 7 years.

When Sharon was first diagnosed with breast cancer, she reached out to her parents, who had moved to another state several years before. Her father started crying and told her that whatever she needed they would provide. Within the next 2 weeks, however, her mother called Sharon to say that they would not be able to take care of the children while Sharon was in the hospital nor would they be able to help her out financially. Sharon's mother had scheduled a knee operation for herself and would not be able to travel; plus she would need to have Sharon's father home to care for her after the operation. Sharon was devastated. She hid her hurt and feelings of betrayal from everyone and put on what she called her "strong woman mask." Sharon believed that her only form of support would need to come from Tony.

Tony had always tried to keep everything running smoothly. He hated conflict of any kind, and strong emotions scared and intimated him. One thing that caused Tony great anxiety and fear was anyone becoming dependent on him. Tony had never believed that he could be counted on for anything. His parents had called him a screw-up for so many years that he believed them. Tony always ran from intense feelings and intimacy. When faced with Sharon's dependence and fear, Tony ran away emotionally. He did not visit her in the hospital or talk to her about her illness. He did a good job of taking care of the children, making sure they were fed and taken to school. But when Sharon hinted about needing him, Tony shut down emotionally and ignored the hints. Sharon eventually stopped hinting.

The cancer treatment and mastectomy were successful. Sharon was declared cancer-free a year after the operation. A triathlon athlete prior to getting cancer, she began training again. Sharon had always been very health conscious. She didn't smoke or drink, she exercised a lot, her weight was always on the low side of normal, and she watched her diet. After her cancer treatments, she cut out all refined sugar and flour, ate only organic foods, and continued a strict and regimented exercise routine. She continued to home-school the children for a half day every day. However, her relationship with Tony worsened. Sharon described a cycle they would follow. Tony would complain about something under his breath, Sharon would try to do something about this complaint, Tony would continue to complain about this thing but never directly to Sharon, Sharon would feel helpless to fix it, Tony would complain more, Sharon would eventually become depressed and angry, and finally she would blow up. These blow-ups usually ended with Sharon becoming violent, and about half the time Tony would respond in kind. When they were not in this cycle, Sharon and Tony lived as roommates who didn't particularly like each other.

Outside of her relationship with Tony, Sharon had a few close friends. These were people Sharon took care of—they always needed help or advice. Sharon said that she loves being able to "be there for people." "There is nothing better than being needed," she added. At times Sharon ran herself ragged helping her friends move, survive relationship difficulties, get through school, and so on. Sharon did not feel comfortable reaching out to her friends when she had cancer because they were all too busy, too overwhelmed with their own lives, or too scared of cancer to help her. Sharon felt it was much easier to cope with everything on her own.

Sharon and Tony divorced about 3 years after her cancer treatment. Their relationship remained contentious. Tony moved in and out of the house every few months. He said that he moved back in so he could be with the children and help out financially. Sharon looked at these occasions as times to work on their relationship and possibly get back together. Because they both had such different agendas, conflicts arose and the destructive patterns repeated themselves. Neither Sharon nor Tony directly addressed the issues that repeatedly came up for them—Sharon would not confront Tony, and Tony would only confront Sharon with passive-aggressiveness.

1. Hans Selye's theory of the general adaptation syndrome states that stress has a direct effect on physiological functioning. Identify Sharon's stressors, both acute stressors and chronic hassles.

2. If nothing changes in Sharon's life, what would Selye predict might happen?

3. If you were Sharon's therapist, what goals would you choose to help her reduce the stress in her life?

When Sharon was diagnosed with a recurrence of breast cancer, she became very angry at her doctors, Tony, the health care system, and her parents. The cancer had spread into her brain, into her bones, and throughout her lymph system. Sharon did not believe that she was going to die. After she took the alternative herbal treatment in Mexico, some of her tumors got smaller or disappeared. She told her oncologist in the United States that she would not allow another operation, but her oncologist refused to have her as a patient if she used alternative medical treatments. The only traditional treatment she allowed was some radiation targeted on a tumor that was pushing against her spinal column, causing pain and paralysis. Since that treatment, the tumor disappeared, but Sharon's overall health went downhill. She believed her poor health was a reaction to the radiation and that she would rebound soon.

Sharon stated that she used to believe that all these things were happening to her as some sort of punishment. She believed that her life was out of her control. When she decided to take control of her cancer therapy and explore alternative treatment possibilities, she felt stronger than she had ever felt. She said that it was interesting that by asserting herself over her cancer treatment all her feelings of anger and resentment toward her parents, Tony, and her friends emerged. She believed that her body reacted to stresses in her life by developing tumors. After a recent fight with Tony, she noticed a new tumor had started to grow in her skull. When she stopped fighting, the tumor disappeared.

4. Using your understanding of Kobasa's theory of hardiness, what do you think is happening with Sharon?

5. If the theory of hardiness is correct, what would Sharon have to believe in order to get better?

6. A therapist working with Sharon told her there is a personality called Type C and that such people are more susceptible to developing cancer than others. He told her that Type C people tended to put other people's needs before their own and had trouble expressing negative emotions. How do you think Sharon felt when she heard these things?

7. If she felt relieved that there was an explanation for her developing cancer, what would be the next step in therapy?

8. If she felt that the therapist was blaming her for developing cancer, what should the therapist do next?

9. If you were Sharon, would this information be helpful to you? Why or why not?

Name _____ Section _____ Date _____

## ACTIVITY 5-1

Selye's general adaptation syndrome begins with a threat that produces an emergency reaction (alarm). If the emergency reaction uses your body's defenses, you enter the resistance stage. This stage uses physiological responses to minimize tissue damage. If the threat persists, the body's defenses become depleted. You then enter the final stage, exhaustion.

1. Discuss how Selye's theory relates to the last month of college classes. What factors might cause you to enter into the alarm stage?

2. If there is no letup from the things causing you to feel stressed, what happens to you in the resistance stage?

3. Have you ever experienced Selye's exhaustion stage?

CHAPTER 5 / EFFECTS OF STRESS ON HEALTH AND DISEASE   43

**Vignette 1**

Claire is a 19-year-old in her first year at a large Midwestern university. She is carrying an overload of 19 units while working part-time as a waitress. Claire has been dating her boyfriend back home (300 miles away) for 3 years. They have often fought during the year because Claire has not come home for weekend visits and has constantly been tired. When Claire finished midterms, she was very disappointed in her grades and vowed to improve her grades by finals. She has been loading up on extra-credit papers and projects in addition to her regular workload. Recently Claire developed a rash on her chest, neck, and arms. She has had a nagging cough for about a month—she says it is just a leftover from a nasty case of the flu. Claire has also complained of feeling on edge all of the time, saying that she has no patience with anything or anybody, easily becomes angry, and cries at nothing. Her physician has not found a medical reason for Claire's rash.

4. Apply Selye's theory to Claire.

   a. Alarm (what are the stressors?)

   b. Resistance

   c. Exhaustion (what's happening to her physical and psychological health?)

5. According to Selye, what might happen to Claire if her life continues in this manner?

6. Describe a time in your life when stress may have affected your health.

7. What recommendations would you make to Claire?

**Vignette 2**

John, a 16-year-old African American male, has lived his whole life in the projects of Philadelphia. Although his mother works two jobs cleaning offices, the family lives just above the poverty line. John's older brother was sent to jail for a gang-related shooting. His brother had protected him before, but once his brother went to jail the gang began exerting a lot of pressure on John to join. John has resisted because he promised his mother that he wouldn't do so. John has been struggling to stay in school. He was diagnosed with borderline dyslexia when he was 8, but he does not meet the guidelines for special education services at his school. John used to dream of getting out of the projects and working as a computer programmer. Now he isn't sure he'll even graduate from high school. He stated that he sees no point in studying because "everybody knows there ain't nothing out there for me."

8. Discuss the sociocultural stressors that John might be facing.

9. According to Selye's theory, what are the consequences of these stressors on John's health?

10. Do you see any solutions to helping John with the stress in his life?

Name _____ Section _____ Date _____

## ACTIVITY 5-2

**Directions:** Think of a situation that is causing you some stress (a class presentation, an exam, a relationship), and answer the questions that follow.

1. Appraise the situation. State the problem, defining it as specifically as you can.

2. Examine your appraisal. Are you catastrophizing, fortune-telling, or mind reading? Is the world really going to end? Will everybody really hate you? Will it really matter in 10 years?

3. Be aware of your defenses. Are you using rationalization, denial, reaction formation, displacement, or some other mechanism?

4. Use your coping skills to reduce stress. List your coping skills (examples are exercising or talking with friends).

5. Now discuss how and when you plan to use these coping skills to lower your stress level. The more specific you can be, the better your chances of really following through.

6. List some possible problems that might prevent you from following through with your plan (for example, getting home after dark from a long day at work and school and not wanting to go running).

7. List solutions to each of the problems you listed above.

Remain flexible! Do not become impulsive. You have created a well-thought-out plan to help you handle a stressor in your life.

Name _____ Section _____ Date _____

# ACTIVITY 5-3

**Directions:** Suzanne Kobasa and her colleagues have found that psychological hardiness is based on three important personality characteristics:

- **Commitment:** How invested we are in what we are doing.
- **Control:** How much personal control we believe we have over what happens to us.
- **Challenge:** Whether we view what happens in our lives as challenges.

For each of the following rate yourself on the three Cs by circling the appropriate number.

1. In my personal life I believe I:

   | 1 | 2 | 3 | 4 | 5 |
   |---|---|---|---|---|
   | am alienated from what I want. | | | | am completely invested. |

   | 1 | 2 | 3 | 4 | 5 |
   |---|---|---|---|---|
   | am helpless or a victim. | | | | have personal control. |

   | 1 | 2 | 3 | 4 | 5 |
   |---|---|---|---|---|
   | am threatened by changes. | | | | find changes challenging. |

2. In my academic life I believe I:

   | 1 | 2 | 3 | 4 | 5 |
   |---|---|---|---|---|
   | am alienated from what I want. | | | | am completely invested. |

   | 1 | 2 | 3 | 4 | 5 |
   |---|---|---|---|---|
   | am helpless or a victim. | | | | have personal control. |

|   1   |   2   |   3   |   4   |   5   |
|---|---|---|---|---|
| am threatened by changes. | | | | find changes challenging. |

3. In my occupational life I believe I:

|   1   |   2   |   3   |   4   |   5   |
|---|---|---|---|---|
| am alienated from what I want. | | | | am completely invested. |

|   1   |   2   |   3   |   4   |   5   |
|---|---|---|---|---|
| am helpless or a victim. | | | | have personal control. |

|   1   |   2   |   3   |   4   |   5   |
|---|---|---|---|---|
| am threatened by changes. | | | | find changes challenging. |

4. In my vision for my future I believe I:

|   1   |   2   |   3   |   4   |   5   |
|---|---|---|---|---|
| am alienated from what I want. | | | | am completely invested. |

|   1   |   2   |   3   |   4   |   5   |
|---|---|---|---|---|
| am helpless or a victim. | | | | have personal control. |

|   1   |   2   |   3   |   4   |   5   |
|---|---|---|---|---|
| am threatened by changes. | | | | find changes challenging. |

5. After looking at the ratings you gave yourself, what have you learned about your psychological hardiness?

6. What changes can you make to improve your psychological hardiness?

Name _____ Section _____ Date _____

# ACTIVITY 5-4

**Directions:** Health psychology focuses on the interaction between physiological and psychological factors that impact wellness and illness. Research has identified psychological and physiological factors that have been linked to good health. Using the checklist below, indicate which of the following are problems for you or someone in your immediate family by placing a check (✔) in the appropriate box.

|  | You | Your family |
|---|---|---|
| Smoking | ❏ | ❏ |
| Heart disease | ❏ | ❏ |
| Cancer | ❏ | ❏ |
| Hypertension | ❏ | ❏ |
| Asthma | ❏ | ❏ |
| Diabetes | ❏ | ❏ |
| Ulcers | ❏ | ❏ |
| Headaches | ❏ | ❏ |
| Digestive problems | ❏ | ❏ |
| Arthritis | ❏ | ❏ |
| Drug or alcohol abuse | ❏ | ❏ |
| Feelings of stress or pressure | ❏ | ❏ |
| Anxiety | ❏ | ❏ |
| Unhealthy eating habits | ❏ | ❏ |
| Minimal exercise | ❏ | ❏ |
| Others (can include chronic hassles, urban living, low socioeconomic status, disabilities, and so on) | ❏ | ❏ |

Name _____ Section _____ Date _____

## ACTIVITY 5-5

**The Holmes Life Stress Scale**

**Part A: Schedule of Recent Experience:** Check your life events in the last year.

|  | Mean Value |
|---|---|
| 1. A lot more or a lot less trouble with the boss | ☐ 23 |
| 2. A major change in sleeping habits (more sleep, less sleep, different bedtime) | ☐ 16 |
| 3. A major change in eating habits (more food, less food, different food) | ☐ 15 |
| 4. A revision of personal habits (dress, manners, associations, etc.) | ☐ 24 |
| 5. A major change in your usual type and/or amount of recreation | ☐ 19 |
| 6. A major change in your social activities (clubs, dancing, movies, visiting, etc.) | ☐ 18 |
| 7. A major change in religious or spiritual activities | ☐ 19 |
| 8. A major change in number of family get-togethers | ☐ 15 |
| 9. A major change in financial state (much better or much worse than usual) | ☐ 38 |
| 10. In-law troubles | ☐ 29 |
| 11. A major change in the number of arguments with spouse (a lot more or a lot less than usual regarding child-rearing, personal habits, etc.) | ☐ 35 |
| 12. Sexual difficulties | ☐ 39 |

**Total for Part A:** _____

**Part B: Schedule of Recent Experience:** Check your life events in the last year.

| | Number of times | × | Mean Value | Score |
|---|---|---|---|---|
| 13. Major personal injury or illness | _____ | | 53 | _____ |
| 14. Death of a close family member (other than spouse) | _____ | | 63 | _____ |
| 15. Death of a spouse | _____ | | 100 | _____ |
| 16. Death of a close friend | _____ | | 37 | _____ |
| 17. Gaining a new family member (birth, adoption, elder moving in, and so on) | _____ | | 39 | _____ |
| 18. Change in the health of a family member | _____ | | 44 | _____ |
| 19. Change in residence | _____ | | 20 | _____ |
| 20. Detention in jail or other institution | _____ | | 63 | _____ |
| 21. Minor violations of the law (traffic tickets, jaywalking) | _____ | | 11 | _____ |
| 22. Major business readjustment (merger, bankruptcy) | _____ | | 39 | _____ |
| 23. Marriage | _____ | | 50 | _____ |
| 24. Divorce | _____ | | 73 | _____ |
| 25. Separation from spouse or significant other | _____ | | 65 | _____ |
| 26. Outstanding personal achievement | _____ | | 28 | _____ |
| 27. Son or daughter leaving home (college, marriage) | _____ | | 29 | _____ |
| 28. Retirement | _____ | | 45 | _____ |
| 29. Major change in working hours or conditions | _____ | | 20 | _____ |
| 30. Major change in responsibilities at work (promotion, demotion) | _____ | | 29 | _____ |
| 31. Being fired from work | _____ | | 47 | _____ |

|  | **Number of times** × | **Mean Value** | **Score** |
|---|---|---|---|
| 32. Major change in living conditions (new home remodeling, deterioration of old home) | _____ | 25 | _____ |
| 33. Spouse beginning or ceasing work | _____ | 26 | _____ |
| 34. Taking on a home mortgage | _____ | 31 | _____ |
| 35. Taking on a loan of less than $25,000 | _____ | 17 | _____ |
| 36. Foreclosure on a mortgage or loan | _____ | 30 | _____ |
| 37. Vacation | _____ | 13 | _____ |
| 38. Changing to a new school | _____ | 20 | _____ |
| 39. Changing to a different line of work | _____ | 36 | _____ |
| 40. Beginning or ceasing formal schooling | _____ | 26 | _____ |
| 41. Reconciliation with a mate | _____ | 45 | _____ |
| 42. Pregnancy | _____ | 40 | _____ |

**Total for Part B:** _____

**Total Score:** _____

**Your Score on the Life Stress Scale**

Calculate your total scores from Schedules A and B, and add them together to get a total score. Notice that even positive events, such as marriage or vacation, create stress. Almost 80 percent of persons who have a score greater than 300 in one year are likely to get sick in the near future; about 50 percent of those scoring between 200 and 299 will get sick; and fewer than 30 percent of those scoring between 150 and 199 will get sick.

Source: *The Holmes Life Stress Scale* by Thomas H. Holmes. Copyright © 1976 by Thomas H. Holmes. Reprinted with permission from New Harbinger Publications Inc., Oakland, CA 94609, www.newharbinger.com

Name _____ Section _____ Date _____

# ACTIVITY 5-6

**Directions:** Review the life changes scale that follows; circle the point total next to any life change that you have experienced in the past year.

## Health

| | |
|---|---|
| An injury or illness which | |
|    kept you in bed a week or more, | |
|       or sent you to the hospital | 74 |
|       was less serious than that | 44 |
| Major dental work | 26 |
| Major change in eating habits | 27 |
| Major change in sleeping habits | 26 |
| Major change in your usual type or amount of recreation | 28 |

## Work

| | |
|---|---|
| Change to a new type of work | 51 |
| Change in your work hours or conditions | 35 |
| Change in your responsibilities at work: | |
|    more responsibilities | 29 |
|    fewer responsibilities | 21 |
|    promotion | 31 |
|    demotion | 42 |
|    transfer | 32 |
| Troubles at work: | |
|    with your boss | 29 |
|    with coworkers | 35 |
|    with persons under your supervision | 35 |
|    other work troubles | 28 |
| Major business adjustment | 60 |
| Retirement | 52 |
| Loss of job: | |
|    laid off from work | 68 |
|    fired from work | 79 |
| Correspondence course to help you in your work | 18 |

**Home and Family**

| | |
|---|---|
| Major change in living conditions | 42 |
| Change in residence: | |
|     move within the same town or city | 25 |
|     move to a different town, city, or state | 47 |
| Change in family get-togethers | 25 |
| Major change in health or behavior of family member | 55 |
| Marriage | 50 |
| Pregnancy | 67 |
| Miscarriage or abortion | 65 |
| Gain of a new family member: | |
|     birth of a child | 66 |
|     adoption of a child | 65 |
|     a relative moving in with you | 59 |
| Spouse beginning or ending work | 46 |
| Child leaving home: | |
|     to attend college | 41 |
|     due to marriage | 41 |
|     for other reasons | 45 |
| Change in arguments with spouse | 50 |
| In-law problems | 38 |
| Change in marital status of your parents: | |
|     divorce | 59 |
|     remarriage | 50 |
| Separation from spouse: | |
|     due to work | 53 |
|     due to marital problem | 76 |
| Divorce | 96 |
| Birth of grandchild | 43 |
| Death of spouse | 119 |
| Death of other family member: | |
|     child | 123 |
|     brother or sister | 102 |
|     parent | 100 |

**Personal and Social**

| | |
|---|---|
| Change in personal habits | 26 |
| Beginning or ending school or college | 38 |
| Change of school or college | 35 |
| Change of political beliefs | 24 |
| Change in religious beliefs | 29 |
| Change in social activities | 27 |
| Vacation trip | 24 |
| New, close, personal relationship | 37 |
| Engagement to marry | 45 |
| Girlfriend or boyfriend problems | 39 |
| Sexual difficulties | 44 |
| "Falling out" of a close personal relationship | 47 |
| An accident | 48 |
| Minor violation of the law | 20 |
| Being held in jail | 75 |
| Death of a close friend | 70 |
| Major decision about your immediate future | 51 |
| Major personal achievement | 36 |

**Financial**

| | |
|---|---|
| Major change in finances: | |
|     increased income | 38 |
|     decreased income | 60 |
|     investment or credit difficulties | 56 |
| Loss or damage of personal property | 43 |
| Moderate purchase | 20 |
| Major purchase | 37 |
| Foreclosure on a mortgage or loan | 58 |

Total score: _____

Add up your points. A total score of anywhere from 250 to 500 or so would be considered a moderate amount of stress. If you score higher than that, you may face an increased risk of illness; if you score lower than that, consider yourself fortunate.

Source: Reprinted from Miller, M. A., and R. H. Rahe. 1997. Life changes scaling for the 1990s. *Journal of Psychosomatic Research* 43(3): 279–292. Copyright © 1997, Elsevier Science Ltd. With permission from Elsevier Science.

# CHAPTER 6

# THE SUBSTANCE ABUSE DISORDER SPECTRUM

Joan is a 53-year-old White female who has been admitted to the hospital for problems with prescription medications. Joan was well known to the hospital emergency staff because for 5 or 6 years she had come to the hospital at least twice a month requesting medication for migraine headaches. Joan had several other prescriptions she took for headaches and low-back pain, but she sought emergency-room care when these medications were not effective. Joan's primary care physician was on the hospital staff and had left standing orders for Joan to be given Darvon should her migraine headaches reach an intolerable level. The emergency-room staff and Joan's insurance company sought to end this practice because they believed it to be an inappropriate use of the emergency-room facilities and not a cost-effective treatment for Joan's headaches.

For several months the emergency-room staff had been concerned that Joan had developed an addiction to prescription medications. Joan's insurance company and the emergency-room physician decided that Joan must be admitted into the chemical dependency unit for an evaluation before they would prescribe additional medication for her. Joan was angry and upset by this decision, but she agreed to a voluntary hospitalization for an evaluation as long as she received medication for her headaches and low-back pain. "I think you guys are blackmailing me into having to be admitted. As I understand it, you are saying that I cannot receive any medication unless I agree to be admitted as a drug addict." The following history was completed on Joan's admission to the chemical dependency unit of the hospital.

## PERSONAL HISTORY

Joan had been married to Ron for 33 years. Ron, 55 years old, was recently laid off from his job. Ron had worked for over 30 years for a company that makes airplanes. He decided to accept a voluntary early retirement benefit package, which allowed him to continue receiving the same medical benefits he had before the layoff. This compensation was a major factor in Ron's decision to accept early retirement. Joan had required a great deal of medical care for her headaches and low-back pain for many years.

Joan and Ron married young and had two children. At the time Joan was admitted for evaluation, both children were married and had children of their own. Their son lived 20 miles away, and their daughter lived in another state. Joan and Ron stated that they are very close to their children and grandchildren. Joan was an only child. Her parents had been in their early 40s and married for over 20 years when Joan was born. They had given up hope of ever having children. Joan's parents both died when Joan was in her 20s. Joan described her father as a soft-spoken, kindly man. "He had a job as a businessman and worked hard," she said.

Joan became very tearful when she spoke about her father. She stated that losing her father was the biggest loss of her life. Joan said that Ron is very much like her father in many ways. She described them both as loving, kind, soft-spoken, gentle, and generous. One of Joan's favorite memories of her father was of him waking her early on Saturday mornings. They would leave the house very quietly and walk six or seven blocks to the Caboose Diner, where they ate pancakes or eggs or cereal.

> It would be just me and my daddy. We called it our date. Mother liked to sleep late in the mornings. Daddy and I were early birds, and we both believed in good strong breakfasts to get the day started. Daddy had this special way of making me feel grown-up. He really seemed to like me. He would ask me questions and really listened to my answers. I know that the answers were sometimes silly or stupid, but he made me feel like they really mattered, and that what I had to say was important. It was three days before my wedding that Daddy died. He had a massive heart attack and died very suddenly. Even all these years later it still makes me cry to talk about him, I miss him so much. Mother insisted that we have the wedding since we had made all the arrangements and we couldn't get our money back on any of the food or cake or stuff. I was in shock, and I think I went numb. I couldn't even talk. I have no real memories of my wedding. I know my uncle walked me down the aisle. I was crying the whole way. Ron says I just had the saddest look on my face and that the tears never stopped flowing. He tried to tell Mother he didn't think we should have the wedding, but she insisted. When mother gets an idea in her head there is no telling her differently.

The whole wedding and reception was a blur to me. The photographer was very kind. He tried to take pictures where my red, swollen, tear-stained face didn't show too much. To this day I can't look at my wedding pictures. They make me too sad. Ron and I had planned to go to New York for our honeymoon. We postponed the trip because Daddy's funeral was the day after my wedding. I know that people thought it was very strange that we had both the wedding and the funeral together. The same people that came to my wedding came back the next day all dressed in black to attend Daddy's funeral. No one knew what to say to us. They tried to congratulate us on our wedding while expressing sympathy. Mother was in all of her glory. She has an amazing ability to be this magnificent hostess. I was just like a wooden doll.

It's interesting that Mother always appeared so perfectly put together in public. She had terrible migraine headaches and used to spend days and days alone in the dark of her bedroom. I know that she took medicine that her doctor gave her, but other than that I'm not sure what happened in that dark room. When she got one of her headaches no one was supposed to make any noise, because noise made her headaches worse. I know that before I was born this was not a problem, because the house was always quiet. Mother never worked outside of the house. However, when I was little I tried my best to be very, very quiet, but you know how little children are . . . well, mother used to get really angry and would lock me out of the house. She always let me back inside before Daddy got home. She told me it was my fault and if I wasn't so clumsy and noisy she wouldn't have to do that. I think Daddy knew, but he never could do anything about it. When Mother got one of her headaches Daddy would fix her tea and toast in the morning and leave it for her. Then he would come home at lunch and fix her a sandwich and coffee, and then he would fix her supper at night. He was very kind to her.

My mother had headaches a lot when I was growing up. Daddy would be the one to get me up and dressed in the mornings. He made my lunch for school, and he would help me with my homework at night and read to me before bed. Mother tried, but her headaches were pretty bad. When Mother did not have a headache, she was wonderful. She would come out of her room and look beautiful. She always wore nice clothes and smelled good. I remember she would get dressed up to go to auxiliary and bridge club during the week. She also liked to have cocktail parties at home with other couples. She could be the life of the party.

Daddy was always kind of quiet. During Mother's parties he would be the bartender and she would be the life of the party. I remember I thought she was very glamorous. She used to drink martinis and scotch. Not together, but at the parties she drank martinis and when there were no parties she drank scotch.

As Joan recalled some of the details of her childhood, she became teary and excited and very animated. She stated that she loves to talk about her childhood, but as she continued to reminisce she became quiet and sad. She stated that some of her memories are very special and many are things that she really doesn't want to remember. She said that she decided to get married so young to get away from her mother. She was ashamed to admit this and had never even confessed this to Ron. She stated that she is sure that her father knew her real reasons for wanting to get married and that knowledge broke his heart and caused him to die. At this point Joan stated that her headache had gotten unbearable and that she could not continue until she got some medication and her pain was relieved.

For several days Joan refused to continue with the interview, stating that her headache was still fairly severe and that she was afraid of making it worse. The counselor asked her permission to speak to Ron and her children. Reluctantly Joan agreed. Ron made the following comments:

Joan is a wonderful woman, who is the light of my life. She is the only woman I have ever loved or ever will love. I hope you can help take away her pain. It makes me so sad to see her hurting. I do everything I can to help ease her pain, but sometimes there is nothing that anyone can do for her. I can't imagine hurting all the time like she does.

When Joan is feeling OK she is a firecracker of fun and laughter. We will laugh and carry on something fierce. She can make me feel like the sun has risen and it's a bright new day! I was feeling really low after the layoff at my work. I had worked there for over 30 years. I wasn't an important boss or anything, but I was a hard and honest worker. I was good at what I did, and I worked hard. I would have liked to have waited out the layoff. I was union, and the union had pretty much promised us rehire status in a few months. But the problem was the medical benefits. Joan needs to go to the doctors a lot. She needs her medicines. If we didn't have insurance, we would go broke. She is really fond of her doctor and doesn't want to start up with anyone new. She was really afraid that if we changed insurances she would be required to change doctors. She says that this doctor really understands her condition. So, because of the insurance mostly I decided to take the voluntary early retirement rather than waiting for them to rehire us. I wish I would have waited because just two weeks after I took the retirement they rehired everyone that was laid off. Oh, well, I just didn't know, and we couldn't take any chances with the insurance.

I'm not sure how many medications Joan takes or what they are. I go out and buy them for her, but she manages her own medicines. I know that when Joan got admitted to the hospital, they asked me to bring in all of her pills. I went home and got them. I was amazed. There must have been thirty bottles of pills! I'm not sure what they all are—I know some of them are for her headaches, some for her back, some for, you know, the change.

Joan has always taken a lot of pills. I know she told you about her daddy dying. From the time of our wedding she started getting headaches like her mother. I don't remember her ever getting them before her daddy died, but you'd have to ask her about that. When they first started it wasn't very often. We had our children in the first 3 years of marriage. First our daughter, Evelyn, and then a year and a half later our son, Adam. They are both very good children. And now they are good parents. When they were little I think Joan only had headaches once or twice a year, usually when times were a little stressful. After the children left home and got married, Joan seemed to get more and more headaches. In the past 8 years she has had more headaches than not. In the past year it is almost constant.

One of your counselors asked me about Joan's drinking. I thought it was a funny question. She's not an alcoholic. She's in here for prescription pills. In fact, Joan was telling me this morning that she doesn't want to be here because she doesn't have an addiction. She is under medical supervision. Surely her doctor, who she sees regularly, would never allow her to become an addict. Joan hates the counseling groups here at the hospital. She says she has nothing in common with the other patients—they are all alcoholics or cocaine users. We are both wondering why Joan has to be here. Joan's doctor told her he can't do anything for her while she's here and that her insurance wants her to be here. She feels stuck. I don't think you all understand what a good person Joan is. She is a wonderful person and a good mother. It distresses me to see her in here. She never takes any drugs that aren't prescribed for her by her doctor.

Joan does miss our nightly cocktails. Every night since we were married she and I would share a cocktail or two and just relax together. It is a tradition. We never get drunk or anything—well, Joan might get a bit happy when we go to parties, but she has never been passed out or anything. We never drink before 5 p.m. unless we are on vacation or at a special brunch or something. We have martinis or old fashioneds or scotch on the rocks. Just a couple. I enjoy being a bartender, and I know just how Joan likes her drinks. We will have wine with our dinner and occasionally a brandy or glass of port before going to bed. But as I said, we never get drunk or anything.

One of the hospital counselors told me that I couldn't see Joan for 10 days to 2 weeks while she was in here. This is really difficult for her and me. We have always been together. We have only slept apart a few times during the whole time we've been married. I know Joan must be suffering so. I wish you would let me be with her. I could help her.

The counselor said that she wanted to meet our kids and talk to them. I said I'd try and get ahold of them. They are both real busy. The counselor also said that I was supposed to go to counseling groups. I don't think I really want to do that. After all, Joan is not an alcoholic or anything. But I'll go if it will help Joan.

Adam and Evelyn came into the hospital together and were interviewed at the same time. Adam, a 30-year-old business executive, owned his own software company and was married with two small children. Evelyn was a 32-year-old artist. She had one daughter and had been married for 7 years. The following is some history on Joan from their interview:

Adam: "I don't understand why my mother is here. What is going on? She isn't some kind of drug addict or drunk. I want to speak to the person in charge."

Evelyn: "I'm glad she's here. I've been trying to tell Daddy that Mom has a problem for years. Of course Dad can't see anything wrong with Mom, ever. Mom has become a kind of zombie. Sometimes when I call I can't even get her to talk she's so zoned out. Isn't she like that when you call or visit? It's gotten really bad lately.

Neither Mom or Dad will talk to me about it. Come on, Adam, remember last Thanksgiving? How can you say Mom doesn't have a problem?"

Adam: "You're making a big deal over nothing. You know Mom gets her headaches and sometimes her medication makes her seem kind of spacey. She isn't a druggie or an alcoholic, she gets headaches and takes prescription medication, for god's sake!"

Evelyn: "Last Thanksgiving is only one of many examples of Mom's problem. She had invited all of us over for Thanksgiving dinner. When she had called to invite us she sounded great, really happy. Well, when we showed up Mom was in her darkened bedroom, and Dad had been up all night trying to cook the dinner and clean the house. Poor Dad. He is such a nice guy. Well, we all managed to pull together a dinner, and then Dad went into Mom's bedroom to see if she would join us. She said she had a headache, but would try. Well, she came out of her room, and you could tell she hadn't showered in days and she looked terrible. Dad said that her headache had lasted for 2 days now, and they had to go to the emergency room for a shot yesterday. I guess the medication was still working, because she was pretty zoned. Daddy continued on with the Thanksgiving dinner as if nothing was wrong. For the first time I think I actually saw how weird this all was. We all were sitting around making believe that Mom was not this total zoned-out zombie. She couldn't even track the conversation. Adam, you must remember when halfway through the dinner she put her head on her bread plate and went to sleep! Daddy just kept on celebrating Thanksgiving. It was so weird. None of us said anything about this woman who was sleeping in her dinner. We talked about the kids' schoolwork, music lessons, football, and the weather. Meanwhile Mom was sleeping on her bread plate!"

Adam: "God, you make it sound so dramatic. Mom just needed to close her eyes for a bit. It wasn't like she pushed all the stuff off the table and laid down in the middle of the table and snored!"

Evelyn: "You know what, Adam? I think that if she had done that that Dad would have continued serving yams and turkey around her, and no one would have said anything! You know what really got to me? It wasn't that you and Dad and I didn't think this was weird, but it was that our kids didn't think it was weird! I got scared that our kids would think this was OK, normal behavior."

Adam: "Maybe they didn't freak out because it really was no big deal. Did you ever consider that?"

Evelyn: "I tried talking to my father about this after Thanksgiving. I told him I thought Mom had a problem, that it wasn't normal to take drugs to zone out for days and days. He told me that her doctor was prescribing these pills and that he knew best and he would never do something harmful to Mom. My dad is so simple and trusting. How do you explain to someone like that that this doctor probably has hundreds of patients and that sometimes doctors are so overworked they seek the easy way out and just prescribe pills rather than deal with a larger problem? I tried to ask him to get a second opinion about Mom's headaches and low-back pain. He told me he had once asked Mom about seeing someone else, this doctor one of his coworkers had said did great things for his wife. But she had told him she really liked her doctor. Dad, being Dad, dropped it. Dad would never push anything with anyone, especially Mom."

Adam: "No one ever told me that Dad thought Mom might have a problem."

Evelyn: "Dad never really put it that way, but he was worried about her. Come on Adam, in the past year Mom has been a total zombie. She's usually stoned on pills. Have you seen her this year when she is like her old self?"

Adam: "I haven't seen them much this year at all. My business has been really busy. But Martine (his wife) has tried to take the kids to see Mom and Dad a couple of times and has mentioned that she's seen Dad, but not Mom. I just figured Mom was, you know, having a headache."

Evelyn: "Now that we're talking about it I guess I need to admit that it has been going on for a few years, but has really gotten bad in the past year. Both of my parents are wonderful people. They are generous and kind, and trusting. I think they are too trusting. They get taken advantage of by people sometimes. I think they trusted that doctor too much, and now Mom's this drugged-out zombie. Her personality changes when she needs drugs. She gets irritable and angry. Mom was never mean or angry before. Dad spends his whole life taking care of her, making sure she doesn't get upset."

After talking to Ron, Adam, and Evelyn, it became very clear that Joan was addicted to prescription medications. Evelyn, Adam, and a counselor met with Ron to discuss Joan's addiction. With the support of the counselor, Evelyn and Adam were able to help Ron see and understand Joan's addiction. Ron was devastated to learn that Joan was addicted to prescription medication and alcohol. They had trusted her medical doctor, and now Ron felt betrayed. He said that he didn't think that Joan's doctor really ever knew how much alcohol Joan had been drinking while taking the pills. When he attended some of the drug classes offered by the hospital, Ron became alarmed at what could have happened to Joan. He learned that the combination of the pills Joan was taking along with alcohol could have been deadly.

Joan was insisting on being released from the hospital. She continued to state that she was not an addict or an alcoholic and that she did not need counseling. The hospital staff, Ron, Evelyn, and Adam all felt that Joan had an addiction and that she needed help. They decided to do an intervention with Joan where Ron and the children would confront Joan with their feelings and concerns in hopes of encouraging her to get the help they believed she needed. The counselor, Ron, Evelyn, and Adam all met with Joan to discuss her addiction. Joan was angry and hurt at first that her family thought she was an addict. She cried and cried. Ron had an especially difficult time not rescuing her. He had spent his whole married life trying to make her happy and to make sure she felt good. This confrontation was exactly the opposite of everything he had ever done. Evelyn and Adam told Joan about her behavior at Thanksgiving and during the year. They told her they were frightened that her grandchildren would never get to know how wonderful she was because she was always so zoned out and that they were afraid if something didn't happen soon she would die. At first Joan just kept repeating that she had these terrible headaches and terrible pain in her back and that she needed her pills to help with the pain. The counselor explained that all of these pills mixed together and then combined with alcohol were deadly. Joan needed to get off the pills and alcohol in order to know how much of what she was suffering was due to the pills or to physical problems. Joan became very scared about not having her pills. Joan said that without her pills she gets edgy and irritable, and it feels like she is going to crawl out of her skin. Those feelings stopped only if she took her pills. The counselor told her that it would be difficult at times while she was detoxing, but that the hospital would give her other medications to help her, and then they would help her learn alternative ways to manage her pain. After hearing all the stories Evelyn and Adam had told her, Joan said that she was ashamed of herself and that she thought that maybe she did have a problem. Joan agreed to go through the treatment process.

The criteria for substance abuse are:

A. A maladaptive pattern of substance use leading to clinically significant impairment or distress, as manifested by one (or more) of the following, occurring within a 12-month period:
   1. recurrent substance use resulting in a failure to fulfill major role obligations at work, school, or home
   2. recurrent substance use in situations in which it is physically hazardous
   3. recurrent substance-related legal problems
   4. continued substance use despite having persistent or recurrent social or interpersonal problems caused or exacerbated by the effects of the substance

B. The symptoms have never met the criteria for substance dependence.

1. Do you think Joan meets the criteria for a substance abuse disorder? Why or why not?

The criteria for substance dependence are:

A maladaptive pattern of substance use, leading to clinically significant impairment or distress, as manifested by three or more of the following, occurring at any time in the same 12-month period:

1. tolerance, as defined by either of the following:
   (a) a need for markedly increased amounts of the substance to achieve intoxication or desired effect
   (b) markedly diminished effect with continued use of the same amount of the substance
2. withdrawal, as manifested by either of the following:
   (a) the characteristic withdrawal syndrome for the substance
   (b) the same (or a closely related) substance is taken to relieve or avoid withdrawal symptoms
3. the substance is often taken in larger amounts or over a longer period than was intended
4. a persistent desire or unsuccessful efforts to cut down or control substance use
5. a great deal of time is spent in activities necessary to obtain the substance, use the substance, or recover from its effects
6. important social, occupational, or recreational activities are given up or reduced because of substance use
7. the substance use is continued despite knowledge of having a persistent or recurrent physical or psychological problem that is likely to have been caused or exacerbated by the substance

2. Do you think Joan has a substance dependence disorder? On what criteria do you base your answer?

3. Do you agree that adults are all responsible for their own decisions? Why or why not?

4. Joan sought out help with her headaches and back pain from someone she thought of as an expert. She trusted his advice completely. Given those facts, what responsibility do you think Joan's doctor deserves in what is happening with Joan?

5. Do you believe that Joan's insurance company had a right to force Joan to get chemical dependency treatment? Why or why not?

Name _____ Section _____ Date _____

# ACTIVITY 6-1

**Vignette 1**

Toby, a 15-year-old White male, smokes three to four joints during a typical day. He smokes a joint in the morning before school and usually has one after school, after dinner, and before bed. He and a friend grow their own marijuana in a greenhouse in his backyard. Toby reported that his parents know he smokes pot, but as long as he doesn't get into anything harder they don't object. Though friends have asked to buy pot from him, he has always refused because he never wants to be busted for dealing. He has an agreement with his parents that they will let him use the greenhouse as long as he only grows pot for himself and his friend. Toby began smoking pot when he was around 9 years old, and it has been a daily ritual for him for at least 2 years. Toby has stated that he doesn't obsess about smoking pot, and if he doesn't smoke it for a while he doesn't mind. He has said that he has never felt any sort of withdrawal and that he could quit any time he wanted to. He doesn't want to quit because he thinks life is better when he's a little high. He said that he's not hurting anyone, and he's doing well in school and has many friends.

1. What diagnosis, if any, would you assign to Toby? Please explain the rationale for your decision.

2. What are your thoughts and opinions concerning Toby's parents?

3. If Toby were 18 years old, would that make any difference in your diagnosis or treatment decisions? Why or why not?

**Vignette 2**

Anthony, a 25-year-old African American male, is happily married with a young daughter. He is a junior executive for a large bank in the Midwest. About 2 months ago, as a reward for past performance and an incentive for continued achievements, Anthony's company sent him to a conference and training session at an exclusive resort in Florida. At the conference Anthony was wined and dined and encouraged to try new foods, sports, and massages. At the conference Anthony met another junior executive who had been singled out as an up-and-coming young star. They became friends and spent time enjoying the resort. This new friend offered Anthony some cocaine. Anthony had never tried any drugs before and was afraid to try cocaine. He resisted his friend's offer for 2 days, but when his friend kept insisting that it was the most wonderful feeling in the world, he decided to try it. Anthony didn't believe it could be very harmful because his friend was successful and intelligent and didn't exhibit any negative symptoms. Anthony tried the cocaine and loved the feeling of power and confidence it gave him. He continued to use cocaine during the conference, and each time he used it he felt bigger, better, and stronger. After he returned home he went through a period of irritability and depression. He and his wife thought it was probably just a post-conference letdown. Ten days after returning home Anthony began asking people if they knew where he might buy some cocaine. Soon he was using cocaine on a daily basis. He now spends a great deal of time during his day thinking about using cocaine and planning how he will buy it.

4. What, if any, diagnosis might you assign to Anthony? Please explain your decision.

5. You are a friend of Anthony's and you believe he needs to be confronted and educated about what he is doing. What might you say to him?

**Vignette 3**

Darla is a 24-year-old Hispanic female who has breast cancer. During the past 2 years Darla has undergone a radical mastectomy, losing both her breasts, and recently began radiation and chemotherapy. Darla has smoked pot socially since she was 14 years old. In college Darla smoked pot frequently but could stop for weeks without any serious problems. She enjoys the feeling that pot gives her and firmly believes that smoking pot has never caused her any negative consequences. The radiation and chemotherapy make Darla nauseous all the time. As a result, she can not keep food or liquids down. Her doctor mentioned to her that marijuana helps some people overcome this nausea. He told her that because of the current laws he could not recommend or prescribe marijuana. Darla decided to try smoking pot and found it helps her greatly. Now Darla smokes pot all day long, even when she is not nauseous.

6. What diagnosis, if any, would you assign to Darla? Please explain your decision.

7. Would it make any difference to you in diagnosing Darla if she did not have cancer? Why or why not?

# CHAPTER 7

# DISSOCIATIVE, SOMATOFORM, AND FACTITIOUS DISORDERS

Lisa is a 19-year-old college sophomore who sought counseling with Dr. Maupin because she felt she might have a problem. When Dr. Maupin asked Lisa what she thought this problem might be, Lisa became rather vague. She stated that she just felt she needed some help. As the interview progressed, it became clear that Lisa had some symptoms of depression and anxiety, but there appeared to be something more involved.

## PERSONAL HISTORY

I was born in a regular, middle-class, White, normal, and nondescript family. I am an only child. My father is a chemist, and my mother is a secretary. I don't know what else to tell you. It was just regular. I was just regular. I was always pretty average at everything. I wasn't really popular, and I wasn't a geek. I wasn't a brain, and I wasn't a 'tard. I wasn't beautiful, and I wasn't ugly. I was just plain old average. I don't ever remember failing at anything. But, I don't remember really ever excelling at anything. Just a plain Jane, run-of-the-mill, average person.

When Dr. Maupin asked Lisa how she felt about being average, Lisa was rather taken aback. "I guess I'm kind of mad about it. I don't know who I'm mad at, or exactly why I'm mad, but when you asked me how I felt the word that came to mind was mad. I guess I'm mad that I can't be special or extraordinary." Dr. Maupin asked Lisa what she'd like to be special or extraordinary at, and Lisa sank into the couch lost in thought for several minutes.
Dr. Maupin: "Lisa, where are you?"
Lisa: "I'm sorry, I guess I got lost in thought. When you asked what I'd like to be special at, my mind sort of drifted off into all my dreams and possibilities."
Dr. Maupin: "Does this drifting off happen a lot?"
Lisa: "I guess. I mean it's not like I ever don't know where I'm at or who I'm with, but sometimes I guess I get lost in my thoughts and people have to call me back. It used to drive my parents nuts. They'd be talking to each other or to me, and I'd drift off. Pretty soon they'd be loudly addressing me. They used to call it daydreaming."
Dr. Maupin: "Does it still happen a lot?"
Lisa: "I guess. In fact, sometimes a bunch of time will have gone by and I will have daydreamed it away. It's not a big deal. In fact I'd like to forget it happened and continue on with this counseling thing." Lisa continued with her personal history.

My parents were rather quiet people. My dad kind of lived in his head. He was a chemist and fit that absent-minded professor image. He would forget what was happening around him sometimes. My mother pretty much ran the world. She was in charge of everything. She was especially in charge of my dad. My mother was constantly making sure he was okay—not the big okay kind of stuff, although she did that too, but the picky okay kind of stuff—you know, that he wasn't wearing plaid pants and a striped shirt or that his socks matched. It was kind of funny because he used to request just black pants and plain shirts so he would know that whatever he pulled out of his closet would match. However, my mother was the one who bought his clothes, and she would try to style him up—you know, sometimes a wild light-blue striped oxford shirt. . . . I'd tease him about taking those huge fashion risks. Sometimes it was pretty funny. My mom would try to buy him something a bit more fashionable. I remember when those polyester leisure suits were popular. Well, my mom bought one for my dad. Now, my dad would never complain about anything my mom bought for him. But, I could tell he really didn't like it at all. Which was a pretty big thing, because he mostly never cared what he wore. So, that kind of tells you how horrendously ugly this thing was. Well, instead of telling my mom he didn't really care for the suit, he hung it in his closet until it was time to paint the house. When my mom was out, my dad put on that leisure suit and went out to paint the house. It was pretty funny. He managed to get paint on the suit before my mom got home. She got upset with him for painting in his new good suit. She figured it was just my dad being an absent-minded professor again. It seemed pretty clear to me at the time that he did it on purpose. Come on, even an absent-minded professor doesn't put on a suit to paint the house! He never had to wear that suit. My mom immediately gave it to Goodwill.

My mom is a control freak. I guess that is what makes her such a good secretary. She is so organized. All the spices in our kitchen are in alphabetical order. As soon as anything gets to a level of half gone she has a replacement right behind it. For example, if the salt gets to halfway, immediately behind that salt container is a brand new container of salt. In all of my life we have never run out of anything! I remember staying over at different friends' houses when I was younger and being amazed that their parents would need to run to the grocery store for milk or bread or whatever. My parents have never, ever had to run to the store for just a couple of things. My mother has major lists. Her grocery list is a strategical work of art. She has items listed alphabetically according to category—like fruits would be apples, bananas, cantaloupe, etc.—then the categories are listed according to the aisles of the supermarket—then each category has a separate compartment attached to hold coupons. On the pantry, on the refrigerator, and on the freezer she has listed what is inside. It is truly a wonder to behold. If she would only use her massive power for good, whole countries could be saved! Just kidding.

I think I am a combination of both of my parents. I have a need for control and am very organized, yet I also have this daydreaming side. You look at my parents and wonder how they have stayed together for all of these years—they are so different. I guess they balance each other out. I don't think I am balancing myself out very well.

At this point Lisa got quiet again and sat staring at the coffee table. Dr. Maupin waited for Lisa to come back into the conversation. After several minutes Lisa seemed to shake herself out of her daydream and appeared embarrassed at having been caught daydreaming again. Dr. Maupin asked Lisa how many times a day she drifts off into daydreams. Lisa replied that she wasn't sure, but it may be a lot.

Dr. Maupin asked Lisa about using drugs or alcohol. Lisa stated that she sometimes drinks at parties, but that's only once a month or so and that she never has more than two or three drinks. Lisa said that she has tried marijuana a couple of times, but never really felt much of anything from it. She dropped acid once and didn't really like the feeling, so she never did it again. "On the whole, I really don't like drugs and I can take or leave booze. If I never had another drink again, I don't think I'd miss it." Lisa didn't believe that her daydreaming got better or worse with drugs or alcohol. She said that she never had a major head injury or trauma. "Sure, I've bumped my head, but I've never had a concussion or blacked out or anything." Dr. Maupin asked if Lisa would be willing to take some psychological tests to help her better assess what is going on, and Lisa agreed.

During the next couple of sessions Lisa took several different psychodiagnostic tests, all of which indicated no psychotic problems—Lisa had intact reality testing—and no neuropsychological problems. The results did not indicate post-traumatic stress disorder or any drug or alcohol problems. Lisa did score high for anxiety and depression on the MMPI-II, but not in the pathological range. Lisa's Rorschach Inkblot Test results were interesting in that they indicated that Lisa had a very active imaginative inner life and tended to view her world and her feelings from a distance.

One of the most interesting test results was on Lisa's kinetic family drawing, which showed Lisa and her parents sitting and reading in their living room viewed from a television screen. It was as if they were in a scene from a television program. When asked about her drawing Lisa replied, "I just felt like this symbolized us. As I look at it now, it is weird. It looks like I'm saying we're all one-dimensional or something. I thought it was kind of creative at the time, but it is kind of weird." Lisa continued her personal history.

I remember being by myself a lot as a child. I didn't have any brothers or sisters and my parents were great, but let's face it, they were not the get-down-on-the-floor-and-wrestle-with-your-kid kind of parents, unless of course my dad was trying to sabotage a new ugly suit my mom had bought for him—just kidding. I remember having imaginary friends a lot—in fact, I had an imaginary friend until I was in junior high school. I don't think I was crazy or anything, just kind of lonely. I would have tea parties and play house with these friends. I remember when I was about 8 I created that whole huge imaginary world, sort of like Narnia—you know, from C. S. Lewis's books, *The Lion, the Witch, and the Wardrobe*. Anyway, I pretty much lived in my other world for at least a year. It was weird because during the time I was really into it, I remember having trouble sometimes deciding which was the real world and which was my created world. I don't think this was too weird. I think I just liked my world so much, and I wished so hard for it to be the real world, that I almost made it the real world. It used to kind of freak my mom out. I finally stopped after she threatened to take me in for counseling if I didn't stop it. After that I used to play secretly a little, and then I guess I just grew out of it.

I remember sometimes during that time feeling like this world was gray and flat. People were so much less interesting and alive than they were in my created world. In all honesty I still think that way. When I go into my daydreams, they seem more vivid. Sometimes when I am not daydreaming nowadays I sort of feel unreal—like a robot. It's almost like I'm watching myself play myself in this world. In fact, I brought you a picture I drew when I was 8 and going through this whole Narnia thing. I was going through a box of old stuff the other night and found this drawing.

The drawing, beautifully drawn with colored pencil, showed a princess surrounded by animals dressed up like royalty. The animals, like people, were talking and standing or having tea. The princess looked very happy. Lisa got very animated as she talked about her drawing. She remembered the names of quite a few of the animals. She pointed to what looked like a fairy floating in the air in the upper left-hand corner of the drawing. When Dr. Maupin asked Lisa who that was, she replied that it was herself. "Remember how I told you that sometimes I feel like I'm watching myself? Well, I remembered feeling that way a lot when I was little. When I saw this drawing I remembered that I used to draw myself watching myself a lot in my drawings. This is exactly how I still feel. There is a real me that is watching the robot me. I sometimes feel like I go on automatic pilot through life."

1. At this point, what diagnoses are you considering for Lisa?

2. What symptoms, if any, do you think are the most significant so far?

3. Pick your top two possible diagnoses. For each of the diagnoses, list what symptoms you would need to see in order to make that diagnosis.

4. What other possible disorders would you need to rule out?

Dr. Maupin asked Lisa to talk some more about her feeling of watching herself. Lisa said, "Sometimes I feel like I'm watching a movie, but it's my real life. For example, I am dating Scottie right now. He's the first boyfriend I have ever had. He's really sweet, and cute and nice. When we start getting physical and I start getting what might be considered turned on I guess, I just sort of feel myself drift out of my body. I can actually see myself and Scottie kissing and hugging. I analyze how I'm tipping my head or how my lips are when we're kissing. I know it sounds kind of weird, but it's what happens. The bad part of this is that I don't feel what is happening with Scottie anymore. All I feel is what the me that is watching thinks the other me should be feeling. It sounds way more confusing than it really is."

Dr. Maupin asked whether Lisa had these feelings only when she's getting sexual or at other times too. Lisa answered, "Oh, I get these feelings all the time when I get stressed. I guess feeling stressed is the key. Like I told you before, I have an uncanny ability to live in my imagination. When things get too weird for me, I can go to my imagination. I guess the reason I'm coming in for counseling now is that it is starting to happen when I don't want to go to my imagination. I guess I'm feeling like I don't have control of it anymore, or that I don't need it anymore. In any case, I don't really like it so much anymore."

Lisa needed to learn how to cope with stress without leaving her body; the goal of therapy became helping Lisa stay in her body all of the time. Dr. Maupin used a cognitive-behavioral approach to help Lisa learn to identify stressful situations and develop alternative coping strategies. Lisa also worked on building relationships where she could trust people enough to let go of the need to control the relationship all of the time.

5. How do you identify stress in your life? What are the indicators that you're getting stressed out?

6. What are some coping mechanisms that you use in dealing with the stress in your life?

7. Are there other areas you would be inclined to explore with Lisa in therapy?

Name _____ Section _____ Date _____

# ACTIVITY 7-1

**Vignette 1**

Tamara, a 54-year-old White female, moved to Seattle about 6 months ago and now works as a cocktail waitress in a bar. When she first applied for the job, the name on her driver's license and social security card did not match the name she was now using. She explained that she was divorcing and changing back to her maiden name. The manager of the bar saw no reason to question her explanation. Tamara was a very hard worker who got along well with the other employees and the customers. Her coworkers liked Tamara but thought she was odd because she never spoke about her past. When they took a break together, Tamara laughed and smiled at everyone's stories but never added any of her own. When directly questioned about her past, Tamara only smiled and shrugged, occasionally stating that she couldn't remember. One day at work, a customer kept staring at her and asking her personal questions, which Tamara dodged. Finally the customer asked another waitress if Tamara had a sister who lived in Montana. The waitress said she didn't know. This customer insisted that Tamara looked just like a woman from Montana that he knew about. This woman had been married with two children and had disappeared about 6 months before. There had been a massive search for her, but nothing was ever discovered. Police suspected the worst because nothing else had been missing except the woman's purse and the clothes on her back.

1. What diagnoses are you considering for Tamara?

2. Select one of your possible diagnoses, and identify the criteria from the vignette that support it.

3. Are there other possible explanations for the symptoms you have identified? If so, what are they?

**Vignette 2**

Lai is a 21-year-old Cambodian female. A survivor of the wars in Cambodia, Lai immigrated to the United States with her brother 6 years ago, and both have lived with aunts and uncles since then. Both of Lai's parents were executed in Cambodia as traitors when Lai was 11 years old. Lai and her brother were forced to live in the hills of Cambodia for 4 years, until they could be safely smuggled out of the country. During this time, she and her brother were cared for by some monks who practiced a type of Buddhism. In this form of Buddhism individuals pray and meditate for hours on end. Lai continues to practice her religion here. While meditating, she has said, she assumes the identity of several of her dead ancestors. "I become these people and cease to be Lai. I become Phon, Mai, and Lui." While assuming these identities she prays and meditates for them, seeking peace and connection.

4. What diagnoses are you considering for Lai?

5. Select one of your possible diagnoses, and identify the criteria from the vignette that support it.

6. Are there other possble explanations for the symptoms you have identified? If so, what are they?

**Vignette 3**

Roger, a 23-year-old Latino male, requested therapy because he is having problems with his relationship. Roger is in a management training program with a large multinational company and is involved in what he states is a very serious romantic relationship. "My life is going great. I have a great job and a lady I love. I can actually see marrying her and having children, the whole nine yards. My problem is kind of strange. I can't remember large segments of my childhood—I mean years at a time. I always knew it was sort of strange, but now it's making me crazy. I feel anxious about what I'm not remembering. My lady thinks I'm holding back on purpose. We'll be talking and sharing, and she'll tell me these stories from her childhood and want me to share. Well, I can't remember. It's like when a movie is running and all of a sudden the screen goes black. Well . . . I grew up in a really wild and chaotic way. We were dirt poor. There was a lot of alcohol and drugs. We lived in a section of L.A. where there are a lot of gangs. Two of my brothers are dead, and three uncles. I don't actually remember how or when they died. I only know this because my sister tells me or my mom will tell me. I can remember some things, usually really trivial things. But the big things are gone."

7. What diagnoses are you considering for Roger?

8. Select one of your possible diagnoses, and identify the criteria from the vignette that support it.

9. Are there other possible explanations for the symptoms you have identified? If so, what are they?

**Vignette 4**

Derek, a 34-year-old White male, was referred for counseling by his neurologist. Derek has had a paralyzed right arm for 6 weeks. After having a battery of medical tests, his doctors do not believe there is a physical cause for his paralysis. Derek is married with two young children—Samuel, 5, and Peter, 18 months. Derek and his wife, Sabrina, have been having marital difficulties for 2 years. Derek was laid off of his job working in a lumber mill about a year ago. Derek has tried to find other employment and has had a series of temporary jobs, but he has been unable to secure permanent work. Since becoming paralyzed, he has been unable to look for work and has been collecting disability. Derek has stated that he had been drinking a lot prior to the paralysis. Depressed about his work situation and his marriage, he had taken to getting semidrunk in the evenings. Since the paralysis, Derek has not had a drink. He said that he was a mean drunk. He and Sabrina would yell and scream at each other, the kids would be out of control, and he would lash out at Sabrina, sometimes hitting her. The night before he became paralyzed, he and Sabrina had been yelling and screaming at each other for a couple of hours while Samuel was acting up and being "a real brat." Derek said, "I'm not proud of myself, but Sabrina and I were fighting, again, and she was poking and hitting me, calling me a loser, Samuel was screaming and grabbing at me, I was yelling. Finally I smacked Sabrina to get her to stop and I accidentally hit Samuel across the head. He flew into the coffee table and hit his head. His head was bleeding all over the place. We took him to the hospital. We didn't tell them I hit him. We told them he fell. I had never, ever hit my kids before. I swore I would never do that—I was beaten as a kid, and I know how awful it is to be hit. I felt lower than low. From then on, I swore it would never happen again. I cried and promised Samuel and Sabrina. I meant every word I said. The next day I couldn't move my right arm. It's been numb and paralyzed ever since. But, the good news is that I haven't had a drink or hit anyone."

10. What diagnoses are you considering for Derek?

11. Select one of your possible diagnoses, and identify the criteria from the vignette that support it.

12. Are there other possible explanations for the symptoms you have identified? If so, what are they?

**Vignette 5**

Brittany, a 24-year-old White female, is a strikingly attractive woman with long brown hair, large brown eyes, and a tall slim figure. However, Brittany seems to try her best to disappear—she wears plain, neutral, baggy clothing; pulls her hair back into a plain ponytail which she tucks into a baseball cap worn low over her face; and wears large sunglasses. Brittany sought out counseling because she states she hates herself. She said that she is so ugly that she wants to die. Brittany has had plastic surgery on her nose several times. She felt that with each surgery she grew uglier. "All my life I have had this huge, ugly nose with this horrendous bump. I feel like the wicked witch of the west. I had my first plastic surgery 10 years ago. My parents paid for it because I was so depressed about my looks I was almost suicidal. My parents and friends claimed they couldn't really see any bump and that I had a nice nose. They are either crazy or blind. The surgeon said he saw a small bump and that he would remove it. Well, I think he made it worse. I used to spend hours every day just looking at my nose. It's like driving by those accidents on the freeway—you can't help but look at all the gross devastation. I tried to disguise it with makeup to no avail. I have never gone on a date because I'm just too ugly. Guys have tried to be nice, but I know they'd just sit there thinking about my nose. I have spent all of my money on other surgeries to fix my nose. This last doctor refused to work on my nose, saying that there was nothing wrong with it and I should get some counseling. I think he's blind. I have an entire scrapbook filled with pictures of noses that are perfect."

13. What diagnoses are you considering for Brittany?

14. Select one of your possible diagnoses, and identify the criteria from the vignette that support it.

15. Are there other possible explanations for the symptoms you have identified? If so, what are they?

Name _____ Section _____ Date _____

# ACTIVITY 7-2

In the treatment of somatoform disorders, it is important to evaluate the situation and explore the possibility of secondary gains. The secondary gains that individuals receive from believing themselves to be sick are sometimes very subtle. Part of the treatment of somatoform disorders is to evaluate for secondary gains and then help the client get their primary and secondary needs met without being sick.

## Example

Mrs. Yamamoto is a 58-year-old Japanese American female. Widowed, she has raised her children alone for the past 20 years. She has worked as a seamstress all of her life. She has three married adult daughters; the youngest was married 3 months ago. According to tradition, all three daughters lived at home until they were married. After each daughter was married, she moved out of her mother's home and into a home of her own. About 8 months ago, Mrs. Yamamoto began complaining of fatigue, loss of appetite, and heartburn. Her doctor ran a series of tests and could find nothing physically wrong. Her daughters became very concerned because Mrs. Yamamoto had stopped eating and was calling in sick to work—she had never missed a day's work in over 30 years. Her daughters are thinking of either having one of them move back home to care for Mrs. Yamamoto or having Mrs. Yamamoto move in with one of them.

**Primary and secondary gains:** Culturally it is not appropriate to have depression or anxiety. By developing physical symptoms, Mrs. Yamamoto is able to experience depression and anxiety within a culturally acceptable manner. Mrs. Yamamoto may be feeling lonely and no longer needed by her daughters. By developing physical symptoms, she receives a lot of attention and gets to feel cared for and appreciated by her daughters. On some level, Mrs. Yamamoto may be wondering what her life is for now that she has successfully raised her children. They have been the focus of her life for a long time. Rather than face the meaninglessness of life, she uses physical symptoms to avoid self-exploration.

### Treatment goals

- To help Mrs. Yamamoto acknowledge and express her feelings of depression and anxiety within a safe setting without needing to somatosize.
- To assist Mrs. Yamamoto and her daughters to improve their communication with each other, thus enabling Mrs. Yamamoto to understand how valued and important she is to her daughters.
- To assist Mrs. Yamamoto in exploring existential meaning within her life.

1. Write your own vignette for a person with undifferentiated somatoform disorder or somatization disorder.

2. Identify the primary and secondary gains the person in your vignette achieves by somatizing.

3. Develop a treatment plan that will assist this person to get those needs met without somatizing.

# CHAPTER 8
# THE MOOD DISORDER SPECTRUM

Nancy is a 44-year-old female whose father is Japanese American and whose mother is White. A partner in a large, prestigious law firm, Nancy decided to seek out therapy with Dr. Tucker, a renowned psychoanalytic psychiatrist, because "my life has all the trappings of success, but at times I feel a sort of void or emptiness."

Though of mixed ethnicity, Nancy looked Asian, with a round, soft face and large, almond-shaped eyes. Her hair was dark brown and about half gray. Nancy was short and plump. She wore little makeup and styled her hair in a plain, soft, shoulder-length cut. Nancy's clothes were expensive and well made, but they seemed to be chosen not to be noticed. All her clothes were in neutral colors with no patterns or accents. Nancy wore little jewelry; what she did wear was conservative and expensive.

## PERSONAL HISTORY

Nancy was the eldest child of three, with a brother 2 years younger and a sister 4 years younger. She was born and raised in Southern California in a middle-class suburban family. Nancy's father worked as a pathologist at a large medical center, and her mother was a nurse until Nancy was born, when she became a full-time mother. Nancy described her family as being close, but different. Both siblings were married with children. Nancy's brother, a pharmacist, was married to a White woman who was an architect. They had two children. Nancy's sister, a teacher, was married to a White man who was also a teacher. They had three children. All of Nancy's family continued to live in Southern California.

An issue that came up early in therapy was ethnicity. Nancy became very uncomfortable talking about it, but said she brought it up because it never got talked about within her family. Nancy reported that she was raised to be White. When asked what that meant, Nancy stated that her family never really talked about or acknowledged her Japanese heritage. Nancy recalled a great deal of shame associated with being Japanese. She reported that she looks the most Japanese, her brother looks somewhat Japanese, and her sister does not look Japanese at all.

Because her father was a doctor, they had more money than most other Japanese families. Because of this and because her mother was White, they lived in mostly White, upper-middle-class suburban neighborhoods.

> I remember looking around my school and neighborhood and everyone was White, so I figured I must look the same and be White, too. I had no one but my father around me who looked like me. I really don't think I had an understanding of what I looked like until I was a teenager. We would occasionally have extended family get-togethers with my father's family—you know, weddings and stuff. It was weird to see all these Asian faces. Most of my father's family were much less acculturated than my father. They still lived a much more Japanese life. My father was the only one of his siblings to get a professional degree or to marry a non-Japanese.
>
> My mother is a beautiful Irish woman. She has auburn hair and green eyes. She met my dad while they were both working at UCLA Medical Center. She had moved out from Boston to the West Coast to attend UCLA. Her family is one of those large Irish families. She is the black sheep of her family. Her family never really accepted my dad or their marriage. Not only was my dad Japanese, but he was *not* Catholic. My mom's family cut her off after she married my dad. She sometimes looks sad when we talk about grandparents and stuff, but she never talks about her family. My mom is amazing in that I think she tried harder than my dad to help us understand our Japanese side.
>
> My dad worked a lot and was not around much when we were growing up. That was pretty common back in the '50s and '60s. He does not like to talk about anything that is negative or painful. So, as you can imagine there are a lot of family secrets and shame. He and his family were in one of those internment camps during World War II. I didn't know anything about this until I was in seventh grade and we were studying World War II. I remember reading about the camps in my textbook and being horrified and then going to ask my dad if he knew about this stuff. I can still see his face, he looked so sad when he told me—and I think he was actually very ashamed about it—that he and his family were in those camps. Because of my upbringing, I didn't ask him anything more about it, and he didn't offer any more information.

I remember trying to wrap my 12-year-old mind around this information and not being able to understand it all. My mother was finally the one who told me a little about what had happened to my dad. My grandparents were first-generation Japanese. My dad was born in Los Angeles, as were all of his siblings, so they were citizens. But I guess that didn't matter back then. My grandparents owned a small farm, which they had worked hard to buy. When they were interned, they lost everything. A couple of my dad's siblings were able to move to the Midwest and live with friends or relatives, but everyone else was taken to Manzanar. One of my uncles served in the 442nd infantry division and was killed in Normandy. My dad was in junior high school when he was interned. After 2 years he was able to go live with some relatives in the Midwest, where he was pretty much on his own. He got into college when he was 16 and went on to medical school. When he graduated from medical school there was still a lot of prejudice against the Japanese, so he was not allowed to treat patients. Because of this, he decided to focus on pathology. I don't think he ever really liked pathology, but he would never admit that.

Every once in a while now my dad might mention something about the camps, but it is usually in the form of a story or general information. There is an underlying way of being within the Japanese culture—you can never complain or feel sorry for yourself. This way of being was definitely part of the way I was brought up. So, you can imagine how hard it is to come in for therapy and sit and whine and complain about my life—it goes against everything I was brought up to believe.

I remember being maybe 7 or 8 years old and having some kids send me some hateful notes. These notes were of swords dripping blood with the words "Die Jap" or of ugly caricatures of Japanese people, you know buckteeth, glasses, etc. I remember being really hurt and scared by these notes, but also really ashamed. I remember hiding these notes in my wallet so my dad would never find them, because they would hurt him. I was afraid to throw them away because I was afraid someone else would see them and know my shame. I couldn't talk to anyone about these things.

I bottled a lot of this hurt and anger up inside of me. My brother acted it out. He was pretty wild and didn't put up with anything from anyone. He kind of had that samurai mentality augmented with an ugly Irish temper. He decided fairly young that he wanted to embrace being Japanese. My parents made a wise decision and decided to channel all of that anger and hostility into martial arts. My brother studied all the martial arts and became very accomplished at all of them. He seemed to relate to the Asian rituals. It seemed that being Japanese added to his life in a way that made him better. He is bringing up his kids to embrace their Japanese heritage. He is the only one of us kids who has Japanese friends or has visited Japan.

I think that because my sister does not look Asian she did not have to deal with any of the negative stuff my brother and I had to deal with. She and my mother are a lot alike. They have the same personalities. My sister is a perfectionist, but she also manages to juggle her career and children. This perfectionism and more than full life make her rather demanding of the people close to her. She expects everyone to share her vision and values. She has a really kind and compassionate heart, but has trouble extending flexibility to those close to her. It is interesting in that my mother is a perfectionist and needs to do things correctly all of the time. She has a hard time allowing people to make mistakes, too. She has her own pace and way of doing things and doesn't like anyone to tell her differently. My mother gets a lot of strokes from being perfect. However, she has a hard time with criticism. She will never admit she may have made a mistake. It's interesting, but I think my mom believes she is Japanese. She has lost her Irish self. She's actually more Japanese than my dad.

I remember when I was really little my mom was always preoccupied with my brother and sister. My mom had three kids in 5 years! Just as one of us was getting out of diapers, another would be born. My aunt came to live with us for a couple of years when I was young. She was a lot younger than my dad; she must have been just 18 or so when she was living with us. She was going to college and spent her free time being a sort of nanny to me and my brother. She was great. I remember thinking that she was magical, because she could do all this amazing stuff. My dad was working all of the time, and my mom was overwhelmed with my younger brother and sister, so my aunt sort of took me under her wing. She's the one who taught me to tie my shoes, skip rope, and ride a bike. After she finished college, she moved to the Midwest to get married. I was devastated. No one really ever talked to me about what was happening, and then she was gone. I remember sitting in my room thinking I must have done something wrong, or else my aunt would never have left. It still hurts to talk about it now. After she left, I was pretty lonely.

My siblings and I have never talked about prejudice and racism. I guess it's that shame thing. I assume they got hit with a lot of weird stuff, too. Because all of my friends were White, I never talked about this with anyone. I do remember trying to tell a couple of my college friends about it once. One was gay and the other overweight. They both immediately went into stories about their own battles with prejudice. I backed away. I remember being confused and then really kind of mad. Both of my friends didn't really understand. My gay friend could chose to just not tell people he was gay, and my overweight friend could diet—I couldn't do anything. I remember someone once telling me that I wouldn't be accepted in Japan because I'm half and half. I guess I always sort of lived with the belief that I would never be accepted anywhere, ever. I know my mom's family sure wouldn't accept any of us!

Sociocultural theorists believe it is extremely important to take social stressors into account when working with clients from minority groups. Acculturation is the process of adaptation through which minority groups identify with the majority culture. There are two major theories of acculturation. The melting pot theory states that acculturation helps people adjust to living in the majority culture by accepting the values and customs associated with the mainstream culture. The bicultural theory believes that adjustment is fostered by identification with both traditional and host cultures. It is important to measure acculturation when working with or diagnosing anyone from a minority culture.

1. How acculturated do you think Nancy is? On what do you base your opinion?

2. Do you think Nancy has acculturated using the melting pot or the bicultural method? Why?

3. What further information would you like in order to better understand Nancy's level of acculturation?

4. How acculturated do you think Nancy's family is? Why?

   a. Her father?

   b. Her brother?

   c. Her sister?

5. What impact do you think ethnicity will have on Nancy's overall therapy?

As I talk about this, I think I'm getting an idea of why I pulled into myself. I guess I see myself as sort of a turtle. I pull into a shell to protect myself from rejection. However, in all honesty, I think I pull into my shell when I don't really need protection. Honestly, I would only get hit by rejection maybe 1 percent of the time. It's kind of a defense against a "just in case" rejection. It's weird, but this prejudice stuff and personal rejection stuff has a way of hitting you when you least expect it. You'll be happily going along, sort of trusting life, and then BLAMMO, right between the eyes—someone hits you with a hateful comment or blows you off or whatever. You're never adequately prepared for it. So, at a very young age I developed a sort of system of protection. But by doing that, I limit myself. I don't allow myself to take risks for fear I'll be hurt. I have never let anyone in close enough to really hurt me, so I really can't understand what I'm so afraid of. In addition to having this shell, I also have a whole arsenal of defenses to keep myself safe.

I don't even know if I'm lonely or unhappy. But I can't remember ever feeling any really strong emotion, including happiness. I guess I feel just sort of numb. I don't think anyone feels particularly close to me. I have a few friends, but they don't really know me. We mainly just do things together—you know, go out to eat, see plays, concerts, etc. We don't really spend much time talking about ourselves; we mostly talk about our work. My friends tend to be other lawyers; some are married, some divorced, some single, men and women. I get asked out on dates occasionally, but always say no. My mom would like me to get married and have children—to her that's the most important thing in the world. The fact that I am very successful career-wise doesn't really count in her book because I'm not married with children. My dad is pretty disconnected and has never said anything one way or the other.

I have another confession to make. This will sound really pathetic. I have been working for my law firm for over 10 years. I have been a full partner for 4 years. I get a lot of vacation time as part of my benefits package, [but] I only take a week or two a year, and then only when I get pressure to do so. I have years and years worth of vacation time stocked up. The really pathetic part is that I can't think how to use it. When I have taken vacation time, I end up at home doing projects or stuff. I tried going to Europe with one of those tours a few years ago and had a miserable time. I really have no friends who I can vacation with. I would no more vacation with my family than have a root canal. I am not a real social person, so it is very difficult for me to make friends easily. And I can't think of anything I'd like to do. I have lots of money, but nothing to spend it on.

My specialization is tax law. School was always very easy for me. When I was a senior at Stanford, I had to make a decision as to what I wanted to do with my life. Up until then I had studied this and that, mainly just dabbling. I was always very interested in medicine. I really enjoyed all of my science and math classes and considered going to medical school. The reason I chose not to do that was that I didn't want to be a part of a system that had screwed my dad. I doubt that he thinks of it that way, but I do. Because of his heritage he had to spend his life poking around dead bodies and analyzing body parts rather than getting to treat patients. I know that logically this would probably not even be an issue today, but I guess on some level I didn't want to be any part of it.

In my family there really was no choice about pursuing an education and a profession. It was unspoken, but assumed. My family was not rich, but my parents had saved a lot of money for all of our college funds. We were allowed to chose any college we wanted to go to and to chose any graduate school. Money was not a consideration. I doubt many people nowadays have this luxury. In my family we never took grand vacations, and my parents always drove their cars until they couldn't be driven any further, and we didn't live in a large house. My parents did all of this in order to save for college. So, you can see why it was just assumed we would go to college. Luckily, all of us kids had the brains to excel in school. Maybe it was that Asian emphasis on education.

I ended up in law school because I was mad at medicine. Stupid. Don't get me wrong, I like law, I'm just not passionate about it. Law seemed the next best alternative. I went to Harvard Law and graduated in the top 5 percent of my class. I was heavily recruited by many firms because I was an Asian, female, tax specialist, who graduated Harvard Law. I never took a lot of pride in my accomplishments—it was all just expected. I don't remember ever enjoying school—it was just something I did. I went to parties occasionally, but never really enjoyed them. I liked going out with a small group of friends, to dinner or the movies. I never really dated during my time at Stanford or Harvard.

I chose the law firm I am with because it was back on the West Coast, close to my family, and it was highly prestigious. I earn an enormous salary and have excellent perks. I'm very good at what I do; in fact, I'd say I am the best they have doing tax law now. Partly that's because I devote my life to my work. I have no attachments or distractions and can focus completely on my work. At times that seems to be enough, but then I wonder. Again, I don't get joy from my work. I get pride from doing an excellent job. I get satisfaction from my work. But I don't get happiness.

I feel flat. I don't cry or feel at all sorry for myself. But, there are moments when I am aware of feelings of emptiness. I guess you would call those feelings sadness. But I'm not sure what I am sad about. I do remember feeling strong feelings of sadness and anger and rage when I was younger. I also remember consciously pushing those feelings down because they did nothing but hurt me. When I pushed those feelings down, I think I may have pushed all my feelings down.

Actually now that I am talking about it, I guess I have always felt rather sad. I've always thought of it as kind of a gray heaviness. I remember looking at other people laughing and getting excited and thinking it was strange that I never did that. There are times when this feeling of gray heaviness is stronger than other times. During these times I have trouble sleeping. I can't seem to turn off my mind and get to sleep, or I'll wake up really early and not be able to get back to sleep. Either way I'm exhausted and kind of cloudy mentally. I find myself eating a lot of sugar and fat and not having the energy to work out; I usually gain weight. These periods last about a week every couple of months. They've been just a part of my life for as long as I can remember.

## TREATMENT

Dr. Tucker referred Nancy for a complete medical examination, during which it was discovered that Nancy had a low thyroid reading. Low thyroid can cause some of the symptoms that Nancy had described. Nancy was placed on Synthroid, a thyroid replacement medication. Dr. Tucker also recommended Nancy try taking Prozac to help alleviate her depressed mood so she could focus on the serious work of doing therapy.

Nancy had sought out Dr. Tucker because of his reputation as an eclectic psychoanalyst. She had heard good things about the doctor from some colleagues at work. Dr. Tucker explained that the way he worked would be to help her understand some of her ambivalent feelings toward important people in her life. He explained that much of the anger she had toward people and situations she had unconsciously turned inward onto herself. When she was able to turn her anger outward, through verbal expression of her feelings, that anger would stop being directed against herself. It was this anger turned inward that was causing her feelings of depression and emptiness.

Dr. Tucker also believed that a large part of Nancy's depression was a form of grief she felt toward the loss of an important early relationship. This grief was different from normal grieving because she was blaming herself for the loss. Nancy's self-blame may have been caused by her absent father, overwhelmed mother, or departed aunt. Since Nancy was the oldest child, she would have been dethroned by the births of her younger brother and sister. Her siblings would have required that Nancy's mother focus on their needs, possibly ignoring Nancy. Nancy may have blamed herself for this loss of parental affection, which in turn increased her feelings of worthlessness and low self-esteem.

Because he was an eclectic psychoanalyst, Dr. Tucker would also prescribe medications to help Nancy, as well as using cognitive-behavioral methods. Some of these methods would be used to help build self-worth through new relationships and goals. Dr. Tucker would also help Nancy explore her need to become self-actualized. Nancy had always lived up to everyone else's expectations of herself. She had never deeply explored the things that would add passion to her life. Dr. Tucker believed that Nancy was asking for help to learn to take risks and to come out of her self-imposed exile.

Because of the nature of psychoanalytic psychotherapy, this would probably take a great deal of time. Nancy would need to commit to coming for therapy at least three times a week for at least a year. This type of therapy is not as long-term or intensive as traditional psychoanalysis, but it is still long-term and intensive. Nancy agreed to all the terms of therapy and seemed happy and relieved to finally be addressing these issues that had troubled her for years.

6. What *DSM-IV* diagnosis would you give to Nancy?

   a. Axis I:

   b. Axis II:

   c. Axis III:

   d. Axis IV:

   e. Axis V:

7. What do you see as the strengths and weaknesses of the psychoanalytic interpretation of Nancy's depression?

8. How would a humanistic-existential therapist view Nancy's problem?

9. How would a humanistic-existential therapist work with Nancy in therapy?

10. How would a cognitive-behavioral therapist view Nancy's problem?

11. How would a cognitive-behavioral therapist work with Nancy?

Name _____ Section _____ Date _____

# ACTIVITY 8-1

Aaron Beck believes that people who are depressed tend to use negative attributions. Depressed people have negative beliefs about themselves, the world, and the future (Beck's cognitive triad of depression). Beck outlined four typical thinking errors that can lead to depression: arbitrary inference; selected abstraction; overgeneralization; and magnification and minimization.

In the activity that follows, each of the four errors is defined. After each definition there is a sample vignette, a list of feelings, a more balanced explanation, and a new list of feelings. After each sample vignette, write out your own vignette reflecting the particular thinking error. Then write out related feelings, a more balanced and logical explanation, and a list of new feelings.

**Error 1: Arbitrary inference. Depressed people interpret neutral events as negative reflections on themselves, often without any evidence.**

Terri received a C on her abnormal psychology exam. Terri was sure that her professor was profoundly disappointed in her performance and now had little respect for her. When her professor walked past her in the hallway one morning and didn't say hello, Terri was certain it was because the professor thought she was a loser.

**Terri's feelings:** depressed, ashamed, stupid, rejected, inferior.

**More balanced explanation:** "I am disappointed in my performance and need to study better next time. Maybe my professor was preoccupied with something in the morning and didn't see me in the hallway. My professor may have been really busy and didn't have time to talk to me."

**Terri's new feelings:** disappointed in her performance, determined.

1. Now write your vignette related to arbitrary inference.

2. Describe the person's feelings.

3. Write a more balanced and logical explanation.

4. Describe the person's new feelings.

**Error 2: Selected abstraction. Depressed people magnify minor events out of all proportion and dwell on the negative.**

Heidi is a 22-year-old female who is completing her first semester of student teaching at a local elementary school. She has been doing a great job. Her students respond well to her, and their parents appreciate her hard work and enthusiasm. Her master teacher has always been very encouraging. On her final evaluation by her master teacher, Heidi received high marks on everything except disciplining students, where she was rated average. Heidi knows that this is an area of weakness and has discussed the area with her faculty advisor, but now Heidi feels like a failure. She is sure she will never get a job because she is just average.

**Heidi's feelings:** disillusioned, depressed, disappointed, ashamed, inferior.

**More balanced and logical explanation:** "I am a really good teacher. The children have all grown and learned and the parents have told me I have done an excellent job. All of the marks on my evaluation were in the superior range except one. I was rated average in the area of discipline. I know this is my weakness and I know I can become superior in that area, too. I need to consult with more experienced teachers and find out how they became good disciplinarians. Being average in one area does not mean I can never be a teacher."

**Heidi's new feelings:** proud, excited, determined, focused, directed.

5. Now write your vignette related to selected abstraction.

6. Describe the person's feelings.

7. Write a more balanced and logical explanation.

8. Describe the person's new feelings.

**Error 3: Overgeneralization. Depressed people interpret any setback as clear evidence for their unworthiness.**

Katie is in her first year at college. It is her first time away from home. She decided to live in a dorm because she did not know anyone else on campus and thought it would be a good way to make new friends. Katie has met several people and really likes her new roommate. One day Katie heard that a group of people that she knew were going out for pizza that night. Her roommate was invited but not Katie. Katie went to her room and decided to stay there for the rest of the weekend. She decided she must be a real loser for everyone to have rejected her already.

**Katie's feelings:** rejected, judged, unacceptable, lonely, abandoned, lost, left-out, isolated.

**More balanced explanation:** "It feels bad not to be included, but there will be other opportunities. If I want to have friends, I guess I need to be more proactive and initiate some fun activities. I'll bet there are other people here in the dorms with no big plans tonight who might want to go dancing or to a movie. I need to initiate some fun and friendships for myself and not just wait for others to do it for me!"

**Katie's new feelings:** left-out, determined, excited, challenged.

9. Now write your vignette related to overgeneralization.

10. Describe the person's feelings.

11. Write a more balanced and logical explanation.

12. Describe the person's new feelings.

**Error 4: Magnification and minimization. Depressed people magnify negative events and minimize positive ones.**

Carl just began working at a new job as a computer programmer. His boss has been very encouraging and supportive. In fact, Carl's boss nominated Carl for a special certificate of appreciation for his very first project. Carl had worked hard on this project and was gratified to see that his work was recognized. Carl has been working equally hard on his new project. When he showed his boss the progress he was making, his boss briefly glanced at it and said, "Good." Carl was crestfallen. He thought he was doing even better work on this new project, but now he was sure that his first project must have been just a fluke or dumb luck. He obviously didn't have what it takes to make it in the business world.

**Carl's feelings:** criticized, defeated, inadequate, vulnerable, unsupported.

**More balanced explanation:** "Hey, I'm a working professional now. I can't expect to be praised and appreciated for everything I produce—this isn't grade school. I know I can do this job well. I know my boss is impressed with my work and my ability. I need to recognize my own strengths and abilities."

**Carl's new feelings:** strong, independent, responsible, able.

13. Now write your own vignette related to magnification and minimization.

14. Describe the person's feelings.

15. Write a more balanced and logical explanation.

16. Describe the person's new feelings.

Name _____ Section _____ Date _____

## ACTIVITY 8-2

In our society we try to teach children how to live successfully. We place a great value on living a worthwhile and correct life. However, usually nobody teaches us how to die or how to grieve. Death is something that is inevitable for all of us. Within our American culture, we have many different ways of grieving.

1. How old were you when you first understood about death?

2. How was death explained to you? Who explained it to you? What were the circumstances surrounding this explanation?

3. In your culture, how do people grieve? (wake? memorial? sitting shiva?)

4. In your culture, are there rules about appropriate grieving for males and females, adults and children? How does the level of relationship—for example, spouse, child, sibling, friend, or acquaintance—affect the rules of grieving?

5. In your culture, when do you think grieving would be viewed as pathological?

6. In your culture, how would pathological grief be handled?

Name _____ Section _____ Date _____

## ACTIVITY 8-3

The right to die has been a controversial topic for many years. The controversy has expanded to include what is now being termed *passive* and *active euthanasia*. Passive euthanasia is seen as allowing a person to die a natural death, that is, not using any extraordinary lifesaving measures to prolong life. Active euthanasia means administering medication to end life. The debate can become even more complicated with the inclusion of such issues as mental competence, euthanasia of minors, and quality of life.

1. Under what conditions would you consider euthanasia for yourself?

2. Have you discussed your wishes with anyone in your family? If so, with whom? If not, why not?

Consider the following vignettes. After each vignette, write an argument both for allowing and for denying euthanasia. (Most people have strong opinions one way or the other; try to understand and explain the opposite side.)

### Vignette 1

George, a 77-year-old male, has inoperable brain cancer. He has been in great pain for the past 2 months. The doctors cannot do anything but try to control his pain. He had told his wife that he wanted to die if he ever became a burden and there was nothing else that could be done for him. His wife is a devout Catholic, and the church forbids euthanasia.

3. Write an argument against euthanasia in this case.

4. Write an argument for euthanasia in this case.

**Vignette 2**

Paula, a 34-year-old wife and mother, was in a car accident that caused her irreparable brain damage. The doctors say that she will never regain consciousness. Her body continues to breathe on its own, but Paula requires feeding tubes and 24-hour nursing care. Paula's hospital bills have already used up all of her family's savings, and her husband is going to have to sell the house and go into debt to pay for continued care. Paula would never have wanted her family to live in poverty, and she had dreamed of her children being able to attend college.

5. Write an argument against euthanasia in this case.

6. Write an argument for euthanasia in this case.

**Vignette 3**

Alice and Frank had a baby boy who was born 3 months prematurely. Doctors say that the baby will die unless they do an extensive operation on his heart and lungs. There is only a 50 percent chance that the operation will be successful. Even if it is successful, there is only a 20 percent chance that the baby will develop normally without severe disabilities.

7. Write an argument against euthanasia in this case.

8. Write an argument for euthanasia in this case.

**Vignette 4**

Eric, who is 30, was recently diagnosed with AIDS. He had been HIV positive for 3 years, during which time he lost his partner and all of his close friends to AIDS. Although Eric has AIDS, he is still basically very healthy. However, Eric has asked his doctor to help him die now before he develops all of the debilitating disorders that result from having AIDS. Eric does not want to go through what his friends and lover had to endure. He says that above all else he wants to die with dignity, and he knows that is not possible for someone with AIDS. Eric states that he is completely aware of what he is asking for and that he has made all the necessary personal arrangements. He would like to die legally, painlessly, and with dignity. However, if the doctor will not help him, he will be forced to seek alternative methods, which are not as clean or predictable.

9. Write an argument against euthanasia in this case.

10. Write an argument for euthanasia in this case.

11. Would you consider someone who wished to commit suicide mentally ill? Why or why not?

12. If Eric's doctor refused to help him and Eric decided to commit suicide, should he be involuntarily committed because he is a danger to himself? Why or why not?

Name _____ Section _____ Date _____

# ACTIVITY 9-1

**Directions:** Working in small groups, fill out the following chart.

| Subtype | Positive Symptoms | Negative Symptoms | Gender Factors | Cultural Factors | Etiology | Treatments |
|---|---|---|---|---|---|---|
| Paranoid | | | | | | |
| Disorganized | | | | | | |
| Catatonic | | | | | | |
| Undifferentiated | | | | | | |
| Residual | | | | | | |
| Related disorders: | | | | | | |
| Schizoaffective | | | | | | |
| Delusional disorder | | | | | | |
| Brief psychotic disorder | | | | | | |

Name _____ Section _____ Date _____

## ACTIVITY 9-2

**Directions:** Working in a small group, discuss the following vignette and answer the questions.

Joshua is a 26-year-old White male. He states that he firmly believes that God talks to people and that sometimes he hears God talking directly to him. Joshua believes God can read his mind and that he knows all of Joshua's thoughts, feelings and beliefs. Joshua states that he has done some very bad things and that the only way he can ever be forgiven is to drink the blood and eat the body of God. Although Joshua freely admits that he has never actually seen or touched God, he knows that God is real and that God loves him. Joshua says that he knows God has a special purpose for him and that he'll know exactly what that purpose is when God decides to unveil His plan.

1. Would you diagnose Joshua with a delusional disorder? Why? Why not?

**Do not read further until you have answered the first question.**

*DSM-IV* states that when experiences are shared and accepted by members of a cultural group they are not considered evidence of a delusional disorder.

2. Why would *DSM-IV* need to make this exception?

3. What are the implications of this exception?

4. What do you think about groups or cultures like Heaven's Gate in the context of the *DSM-IV* exception?

5. What aspects of your culture or of groups that you belong to might someone from another culture view as delusional?

CHAPTER 9 / THE SCHIZOPHRENIAS AND OTHER PSYCHOTIC DISORDERS

Name _____ Section _____ Date _____

# ACTIVITY 9-3

**Directions:** Schizophrenic thought disorder can create delusions, "word salads," and unique speech patterns. Read through the following vignette and identify examples of the various thought and speech patterns used by some people with schizophrenia:

I was reading a magazine today and found the section that was secretly written just for me by Tom Brokaw. I know this because he told me he would tell me special things during the news last night—he knows that I am very, very smart and will be able to solve some of the world's problems if I can only get the needed information. Sometimes I don't read the paper because Barbara Walters doesn't want me to know special things—so she will take my thoughts right out of my head, and I will forget I am supposed to have special messages sent to me. Or sometimes she'll make me think that Tom is not my special friend. She even put a secret high-powered thought transmitter into my brain.

Today is the day that I say March, April and May without delay, if I may say. High-powered transmitters permitters me to know no way. Yesterday was a rain delay—a damp, lamp. I like the news, but sometimes it stinks—pnews!

Yellow . . . radios . . . radishes, clocks that socks . . . homework . . . copyright . . . p-u!

Write down some examples of the following:

1. Delusions of being controlled

2. Loose association

3. Thought broadcasting

4. Thought insertion

5. Thought withdrawal

6. Neologism

7. Clang association

8. Perseveration

9. Word salad

CHAPTER 9 / THE SCHIZOPHRENIAS AND OTHER PSYCHOTIC DISORDERS 125

Name _____ Section _____ Date _____

## ACTIVITY 9-4

**Please do not read until you are told to do so.**

Get into groups of four.

Decide which person will be the subject.

Decide which person will be the reader/recorder.

**Once you have made these decisions, you may continue reading these directions.**

The subject should sit down facing the reader. The other two group members should sit close to the subject, on either side of him or her.

The reader will give the subject tasks and then record answers or behaviors.

The two other group members will provide auditory hallucinations: You should talk directly into the subject's ear. You may ramble, give directions, sing, read, or make up nonsense words. You should talk to the subject continually.

**When you have finished Part 1, change roles and continue on to Part 2 using the same format. Once you have finished Part 2, complete the worksheet.**

Turn the page and begin with Part 1.

## ACTIVITY 9-4 (continued)

### PART 1

**Directions for Reader 1:** Read the following directions to the subject. The time in parentheses is the amount of time you should allow the subject to complete the task.

Take out a piece of paper. (30 seconds)

Get a pen or pencil. (30 seconds)

Write your name, address, and phone number on the paper. (60 seconds)

In your head, add 365 + 147. Write down your answer. (30 seconds)

Draw a star in the upper right corner of the paper. (30 seconds)

Write down what you ate for breakfast this morning and for dinner last night. (30 seconds)

Write down how many hours there are in a week. (30 seconds)

Draw a little girl on your paper in the lower left corner. (90 seconds)

Listen to these directions carefully, and then follow the directions. Listen to all the directions before starting the activities.

> Stand up and show us eight fingers.
> Bend down and touch your right foot.
> Turn to the right three times.
> Rub your head twice.
> Clap your hands four times.
> Touch your left ear with your right little finger.
> Sit down and show us nine fingers and wave bye-bye.

OK, the directions are now finished. You may begin.

On the back of the paper write the pledge of allegiance. (180 seconds)

I am going to read you a list of 10 things. After I finish reading you the list, I will wait 30 seconds. Then I want you to tell me as many of the 10 things as you can remember.

**List:**
fun, shoe, tree, door, beehive, kindling, angles, fence posts, machine gun, chicken

# ACTIVITY 9-4 *(continued)*

## PART 2

**Directions for Reader 2:** Read the following directions to the subject. The time in parentheses is the amount of time you should allow the subject to complete the task.

Take out a sheet of paper and a pencil or pen. (30 seconds)

Write down what is in the recipe for chocolate chip cookies. (60 seconds)

Add 469 + 133 in your head. Write your answer on your sheet of paper. (30 seconds)

Write your name, address, and phone number on the paper. (60 seconds)

Write six states whose names begin with vowels. (180 seconds)

Write the first three lines of the song "Silent Night." (120 seconds)

Listen to these directions carefully, and then follow the directions. Listen to all the directions before starting the activities.

>    Tap your left elbow on the desk five times.
>    Lift your right foot off the floor and hold it up for 10 seconds.
>    Bring your left foot up to touch you right foot before you put them both back down on the floor.
>    Stand up and touch your neck, left wrist, right calf.
>    Walk seven steps and turn around.
>    Shake the hand of the person on your right.
>    Sit down, whistle, and give us the "OK" sign.

OK, the directions are now finished. You may begin.

List four criteria for depression. (60 seconds)

Draw a cat in the lower left corner of the paper. (60 seconds)

I'm going to read you a list of 10 things. After I finish reading you the list, I will wait 30 seconds. Then I want you to tell me as many of the 10 things as you can remember.

**List:**
croissant, socks, cherries, knob, fly, marshmallows, god, white, spine, eggs

## ACTIVITY 9-4 *(continued)*

1. Quickly write down what you thought and felt about this exercise in general.

2. How would you feel about having these hallucinations?

3. How might having hallucinations affect your ability to go to school? Could you work?

4. How might having hallucinations affect your ability to be in relationships?

5. Would you be willing to have a blunted or flat affect if you could get rid of these hallucinations? Why or why not?

6. Would you be willing to risk a serious blood disorder or tardive dyskinesia in order to control these hallucinations? Why or why not?

Name _____ Section _____ Date _____

## ACTIVITY 9-5

**Directions:** Work in pairs or in small groups on the following vignettes. Focus on using *DSM-IV* diagnostic criteria. Remember it is important to get an accurate understanding of the presenting problem, precipitating event, premorbid functioning, and current level of client safety. Make suggestions on how you might most successfully gather the information you need in order to make an accurate diagnosis. If you have time, speculate on what therapy you might recommend.

### Vignette 1

Julian is a 23-year-old male who has not been able to hold down a job or attend school. He lives alone and has no contact with friends or family. You are a world-famous psychotherapist. Julian was brought in to see you because a clerk at the 7-11 became afraid when she saw he had some knives in his coat pockets. He refuses to sit down and paces back and forth in your office. He makes little or no eye contact with you and continually hits his thighs with his fists. He mumbles to himself and seems to become irate or angry as he mumbles and then quietly continues to pace. He tells you he can't remember ever not being like this. He can't remember friends or family.

1. What five questions would you like Julian to answer?

2. What are your major concerns?

3. What diagnoses would you want to rule out?

4. How would you proceed in treating Julian?

**Vignette 2**

You are a therapist who specializes in working with the elderly. Mary is a 60-year-old woman whose daughter brought her to see you when she became concerned over her mother's recent behaviors. Mary says she is sad. When asked about her sadness, she states that her deceased husband comes to speak to her every night and tells her how sad he is not to be with her any longer. Mary states she misses her husband and has been unable to eat or sleep much in the past couple weeks.

1. What further information do you need in order to make a diagnosis?

2. Which diagnoses do you consider? Why?

3. Would it make any difference in your diagnosis if Mary's husband had died six months ago? Two years ago? Twenty years ago?

4. Do you have any specific ethical concerns?

5. How would you proceed in treating this case?

132   CHAPTER 9 / THE SCHIZOPHRENIAS AND OTHER PSYCHOTIC DISORDERS

**Vignette 3**

You are a counselor working at the university counseling center. Todd is a 20-year-old college student who was brought to your office by campus security. They had a call from his mother stating that his father needed emergency surgery and they had been unable to contact Todd for the past several days. Campus security went to Todd's room and found it a mess. There were trash and old food containers all over. Todd had not been to class in 2 weeks. Neighbors stated they had heard Todd fighting with someone—he was yelling and screaming. Oddly, though, they did not see anyone with Todd or hear any other voices. When the campus police told Todd about his father, he began giggling and repeating, "sick father, why bother?"

1. What diagnoses do you consider for Todd?

2. What evidence do you have to support your diagnosis?

3. How would you treat Todd?

4. Are there any specific ethical issues you might need to address in treating Todd?

**Vignette 4**

You are a high school guidance counselor. Harold is an 18-year-old Native American high school senior. His teacher has referred him to you because he has been talking about visions he has seen and spirits that he talks with about many different things. His teacher became concerned about Harold after hearing him tell some friends that he was talking to spirits of the dead, who were instructing him to go off into the mountains by himself. Harold says he often talks to these spirits and receives guidance and comfort from their presence.

1. What more would you want to know before making a diagnosis?

2. What diagnosis would you make? Why?

3. Would your diagnosis be different if Harold was White? Why?

4. Are there any ethical issues you might need to address concerning this case?

Name _____ Section _____ Date _____

## ACTIVITY 10-1

Review the general diagnostic criteria for a personality disorder.

A. An enduring pattern of inner experience and behavior that deviates markedly from the expectations of the individual's culture. This pattern is manifested in two (or more) of the following areas:
   (1) cognition (i.e., ways of perceiving and interpreting self, other people, and events)
   (2) affectivity (i.e., the range, intensity, lability, and appropriateness of emotional response)
   (3) interpersonal functioning
   (4) impulse control
B. The enduring pattern is inflexible and pervasive across a broad range of personal and social situations.
C. The enduring pattern leads to clinically significant distress or impairment in social, occupational, or other important areas of functioning.
D. The pattern is stable and of long duration and its onset can be traced back at least to adolescence or early adulthood.
E. The enduring pattern is not better accounted for as a manifestation or consequence of another mental disorder.
F. The enduring pattern is not due to the direct physiological effects of a substance (e.g., a drug of abuse, a medication) or a general medical condition (e.g., head trauma).

Using the above criteria, identify possible personality disorders in the following vignettes.

**Vignette 1**

John, a 28-year-old White male, has constantly called the community hotline to warn the people of important things. John works in a manufacturing plant and lives with his mother. John has been calling the hotline for 2 years. Each time he calls, he warns the hotline worker that "things are in the mix and about to hit the fan." When hotline workers try to get further information, John gives a monologue about a vast galactic conspiracy that is in the making. He says that he's calling to warn people to make sure they wrap their heads in aluminum foil at night to protect them from the rays of the conspiracy. John does not appear to be the least bit put off by people's reaction to his beliefs. He states he has had this knowledge since he was about 10 years old. He states he does not want help or need therapy; he is just sharing information in order to warn people. When asked about his personal life, John becomes vague and reluctant to talk. He is only willing to discuss the conspiracy. However, two or three times a hotline worker has been able to engage John in a brief dialogue concerning his work and family.

1. What *DSM-IV* diagnosis might you give to John?

2. On what criteria do you base your diagnosis?

**Vignette 2**

Lea is a 34-year-old White female who has come for therapy because her boyfriend threatened to end their relationship unless Lea got help. Lea came into her first session dressed in a short leather minidress with a zipper that extended up the front. Her zipper was undone at the neckline so that her breasts were almost totally exposed and undone at the hemline so that almost all of her thigh was exposed. She was an attractive woman who wore an excessive amount of makeup; whose hair was curled, sprayed, and colored; and who wore a lot of diamond and gold jewelry. Lea expressed disappointment that her therapist would be a woman, but then reached out and rubbed the therapist's arm, telling her she was sure it would be fine, because she could tell the therapist was great. Lea said her boyfriend was mad at her because he discovered that she had had an affair with one of his best friends. She had also had an affair with another of his friends, a person she used to work with, and her boss. Lea then began sobbing, stating that it really wasn't her fault, it was just that she had trouble saying no. She then became angry and said she wouldn't be in this mess if she could make some girlfriends, but that women were always jealous of her and never wanted to be her friends. She then became very seductive, leaning in and touching the therapist, saying she was sure that they could be friends because she could tell the therapist was a woman who was secure in herself and wouldn't get jealous. She then started chatting about a new hairstylist she liked a lot.

3. What *DSM-IV* diagnosis would you give to Lea?

4. On what criteria do you base your diagnosis?

5. What factors would you need to see to make the diagnosis of:

   a. Histrionic personality disorder?

   b. Narcissistic personality disorder?

   c. Borderline personality disorder?

**Vignette 3**

Amy is a 24-year-old Asian female. She appears very soft-spoken and quiet. Her psychology professor wondered whether Amy might benefit from counseling because she never talks in class. When any small-group or class discussion takes place, Amy seemed to shrink into a corner and try to become invisible. Amy's professor believed that the only reason she is in the class is that the course is required of all psychology majors. The professor asked Amy to come by her office and talk. When Amy showed up, she looked like she was about to cry. The professor spent the entire time reassuring Amy that nothing was wrong and that she only wanted to get to know Amy better. Amy briefly talked about herself and told the professor that she would like to get to know some of the other students better, but that class discussions were very difficult for her.

6. What *DSM-IV* diagnosis might you give to Amy?

7. On what criteria do you base your diagnosis?

8. What role might Amy's Asian heritage play in her situation?

9. After carefully considering Amy's culture, would you change your diagnosis? Why or why not?

Name _____ Section _____ Date _____

## ACTIVITY 10-2

Many psychodynamic theorists believe that the narcissistic personality disorder is developed in order to compensate for a fragile sense of self-esteem. People with this disorder did not receive adequate or appropriate parental support and approval. Write a short vignette describing the childhood of a 20-year-old White male who has narcissistic personality disorder. Consider such issues as:

- What his parents were like.
- What his childhood was like.
- Describe an incident when this person needed to compensate for inadequate parenting by developing a grandiose sense of self.
- How this grandiose sense of self affects his relationships, career, mood, and so on, now that he is an adult.

*Be creative!*

Some people believe that the narcissistic personality is fostered by our society. Social learning theorists and some cognitive-behavioral theorists believe that today's children are growing up with an exaggerated sense of their own abilities, future, and self. Part of this narcissistic phenomenon may be evident in the sense of entitlement many young people seem to exhibit.

1. Discuss the forces you see within our society that may be fostering narcissistic personality disorder in young people.

2. How might television and the media reinforce or foster this grandiose sense of self? Give some examples.

3. For many years now, elementary schools have been focusing on building up a child's self-esteem. Parents have been taught to build self-esteem in their children. At what point do you think a healthy sense of self becomes narcissistic and self-defeating? Or does it?

Name _____  Section _____  Date _____

## ACTIVITY 10-3

**Directions:** For each item, circle the letter corresponding to the statement that best describes your preference or opinion. There are no right or wrong answers. Be as honest as possible.

1. A. I would like a job that requires a lot of traveling.
   B. I would prefer a job in one location.

2. A. I am invigorated by a brisk, cold day.
   B. I can't wait to get indoors on a cold day.

3. A. I get bored seeing the same old faces.
   B. I like the comfortable familiarity of everyday friends.

4. A. I would prefer living in an ideal society in which everyone is safe.
   B. I would have preferred living in the unsettled days of our history.

5. A. I sometimes like to do things that are a little frightening.
   B. A sensible person avoids activities that are dangerous.

6. A. I would not like to be hypnotized.
   B. I would like to have the experience of being hypnotized.

7. A. The most important goal of life is to live it to the fullest and experience as much as possible.
   B. The most important goal of life is to find peace and happiness.

8. A. I would like to try parachute-jumping.
   B. I would never want to try jumping out of a plane, with or without a parachute.

9. A. I enter cold water gradually, giving myself time to get used to it.
   B. I like to dive or jump right into the ocean or a cold pool.

10. A. When I go on vacation, I prefer the comfort of a good room and bed.
    B. When I go on vacation, I prefer the change of camping out.

11. A. I prefer people who are emotionally expressive, even if they are a bit unstable.

    B. I prefer people who are calm and even-tempered.

12. A. A good painting should shock or jolt the senses.

    B. A good painting should give one a feeling of peace and security.

13. A. People who ride motorcycles must have some kind of unconscious need to hurt themselves.

    B. I would like to drive or ride a motorcycle.

Here are the scoring key and norms.
Count one point for each of the following items:

| | |
|---|---|
| 1. A | 8. A |
| 2. A | 9. B |
| 3. A | 10. B |
| 4. B | 11. A |
| 5. A | 12. A |
| 6. B | 13. B |
| 7. A | |

1–3 points: very low on sensation-seeking
4–5 points: low
6–9 points: average
10–11 points: high
12–13 points: very high

Source: Farley, F. (1986). World of the Type T personality. *Psychology Today, 20,* 45–52. Credit: Zuckerman, M. (1978, Feb.). Search for high sensation: sidebar: Are you a high or low. *Psychology Today Magazine.* Copyright © 1978 Sussex Publishers, Inc. Reprinted with permission from *Psychology Today Magazine.*

# CHAPTER 11

# INTELLECTUAL AND COGNITIVE DISORDERS

Mary, a 58-year-old White female, has been married to Don for 38 years. They have two children who are married with families of their own. Their son Andrew lives across the country. He, his wife, and two children visit Mary and Don at Christmas and for a week in the summer. Their daughter Angela lives with her husband and son about 20 miles from Mary and Don. Don describes their family as close and loving. They see Angela and her family every Sunday and talk to Andrew and his family at least once a week.

## PERSONAL HISTORY

Mary and Don were referred by their family doctor to Dr. Kraus for psychological evaluation and counseling. Their family doctor stated that he had run a multitude of tests and found no conclusive medical reason for Mary's symptoms. Their family doctor would continue to monitor Mary's medical condition, but wanted Mary and Don to begin counseling with Dr. Kraus to help them adjust to what appeared to be early-onset Alzheimer's disease. Don had originally taken Mary in to see her doctor because Mary had begun to forget names of friends and family and she seemed to be "changing." When Don was asked to explain further, he stated the following:

Mary was always the kindest woman in the world. She never had a mean or nasty thing to say about anybody. She then had started to talk about people being out to get her. She has become kind of angry and irritable all of the time. I have also noticed that Mary would spend hours just sitting in a chair looking out the window. She doesn't read or watch television, she just sits. Or sometimes she will pace back and forth wringing her hands and talking to herself, just kind of mumbling about how people are out to get her. I was really scared about what was happening to her. I don't know what she does all day. I work, and sometimes when I come home she's still wearing her nightgown, and the house is a mess. Mary was always an immaculate housekeeper. She loved to have the house just sparkle. Another strange thing that happened was that she seemed to kind of drift off while we were talking. For example, last night I was telling her a story about our friends Bob and Nancy. We've been friends with them for twenty years. Well, Bob is really a card, and I was telling Mary about Bob's latest adventure, and I was laughing and talking, and, well, Mary got this funny look on her face and asked me who Bob was! I thought she was kidding me. But as I looked at her face, she was serious. She honestly couldn't remember who Bob was. Well, I got scared and stopped talking. Mary just sat down in her chair and stared out of the window. Later last night as we were going to bed she asked me how Bob and Nancy were doing and said that she'd like to have them over for a barbecue soon. This kind of thing has been happening a lot lately.

Mary used to love to read. She would read anything and everything. For the past few months, I don't think she's even opened up the paper. It is strange. In fact, the other day when we were driving to our daughter's house we passed a sign for a new restaurant. Well, Mary was looking at the sign and asked what the word was—well, it was Ponderosa. She then told me she had never seen that word before. Now I know she must have seen that word before. It was really strange.

When I took her to her doctor, he asked me a lot of questions about accidents, fevers, drinking, and such. I'm not sure what he was looking for. Mary has never been a drinker. In fact, if she has one glass of wine or champagne a year that's a lot for her. So, I guess he was able to decide that whatever is going on with her is not related to alcohol. Her father had a stroke when he was 76 years old. He recovered some, but was never the same as he was before the stroke. He was a nice man, but he smoked two packs a day. He said he smoked for 60 years. He was amazed that he never got lung cancer, because he said he smoked like a chimney.

Mary's mother died a few years ago of breast cancer. She was diagnosed with the cancer in November and was dead by March. It was pretty quick. It was tough on Mary and her sisters; they were all really close to her mother.

Mary's doctor ran all sorts of different tests on Mary. They x-rayed her head, MRI'ed her head, PET-scanned her head, and all sorts of other things. The doctor said he wanted to make sure it wasn't a tumor or a blood clot or an injury of some kind. When they couldn't see any of those things, they decided it must be Alzheimer's disease. It was a difficult diagnosis because Mary is really young to be having this disease.

**Features of Alzheimer's disease**

1. **Forgetfulness:** Memory loss is the major symptom of Alzheimer's disease. In the early stage, people might lose the ability to remember names, places, dates. As the disease progresses, they forget more recent and memorable material. It is not unusual for people with Alzheimer's to be able to remember incidents from their childhood, but forget where they are now or what they ate for supper.
2. **Sleep problems:** There may be problems falling asleep or staying asleep.
3. **Suspicion, paranoia, and psychosis:** People with Alzheimer's might lose contact with reality. Delusions and hallucinations are common. Suspicious and paranoid beliefs might occur.
4. **Agitation or aggression:** The person with Alzheimer's might become hostile or aggressive. Common behaviors include pacing, yelling, or throwing things.
5. **Wandering:** Person's with Alzheimer's might become restless, wandering away and then not being able to remember how to get back home.
6. **Aphasia:** People with Alzheimer's might have problems understanding written or spoken words or have trouble finding words.
7. **Apraxia:** People with Alzheimer's might develop difficulty dressing themselves, writing, or even using utensils.
8. **Depression:** Depression can be common.

## MARY'S DESCRIPTION

I know there is something really wrong with my head. Today is a good day. Yesterday was a bad day. My daughter Angela came over to visit with her family. I love it when they come to visit. Angela was always the light of my life. She is such a good daughter. For years now we have been more like best friends than like mother and daughter. Well, yesterday they came over, and I couldn't remember her name. I tried and tried to remember, I just couldn't. I was mortified. I tried to hide the fact that I couldn't remember, but the more I tried the worse it got. I know I was getting really upset. I was trying so hard to remember. I know that Don and Angela had no idea what was making me so upset. I was wringing my hands together and getting upset. Finally, I started to cry. Angela asked me what was wrong, and I told her I couldn't remember her name, and I was so embarrassed.

Well, she was just the nicest about it. She told me that everyone forgets things. That it happens to her all of the time. Well, it made me feel better, but I know that most people don't forget things like that.

I told Don the other day that I was getting tired of volunteering at the church and that I was going to quit. I have volunteered to teach Sunday school for twentysome odd years now. I also work in the church office two mornings a week. The truth of it is I have been having more and more trouble remembering what I am supposed to be doing and how to do things. I can't remember the children's names I have been teaching. I feel like my brain has stopped working. I know that people at the church talk about how stupid I am. I know they were just looking for a way to get me out of there. So, I quit.

Sometimes it feels like my memory is behind this glass wall. You know, the kind of glass walls they use in bathrooms. The glass is clear, but it has ripples so it distorts things. Well, I feel like I can almost see what I can't remember, I know that it is there, but the glass is just too rippled for me to clearly make it out. It's very frustrating. Sometimes, I must confess, I get really angry about it.

I'm not sure when it started, but I think it was a couple of years ago. Today is a really good day. On bad days I feel like I am alone and enclosed by those wrinkly glass walls. When I feel like that I just want to curl up and die.

One month later Don brought Mary to her appointment. Mary had been driving herself to her appointments prior to that. Don said that Mary wasn't doing very well that day—and hadn't been doing well for a few days. Four days ago Mary had gone to the market. She was gone for 3 hours. Don was frantic. He called Angela, and they called the police and the market. The manager at the market remembered seeing Mary at the market and thought she had left a couple of hours before Don called. However, the manager did report that there was a full basket of groceries left in one of the aisles that he thought might have been Mary's. A police officer found Mary about 2 miles from home. She was sitting in her car on the side of the road crying. She couldn't remember how to get home. When the police officer brought Mary home, she didn't remember going to the market. Since that time, Don has driven Mary everywhere.

As Don recounted this episode, Mary sat in a chair wringing her hands and looking frightened. Dr. Kraus asked Mary how she was feeling. Mary cringed away from him. She stated that she didn't know him. Dr. Kraus tried to gently remind her of the times they spent together talking—they had seen each other at least once a week for over a year. Dr. Kraus tried his best to help her feel less afraid and anxious. Mary just kept repeating that she didn't know him.

Don stated that this was the worst that Mary had ever been. He thought that maybe she was traumatized by being lost. Don started to get teary-eyed and stated that he wasn't sure he could take it. Dr. Kraus asked Mary if she would mind if he talked to Don today. Mary stated she didn't know Dr. Kraus. Dr. Kraus asked one of the interns to come and take Mary into the next room and to stay with her. Mary was compliant and willing to go with the intern. She continued to look scared and wary, but didn't seem to mind leaving Don with Dr. Kraus.

As soon as Mary left the room, Don began crying. Dr. Kraus let him cry until Don was ready to talk. Don stated that this was the worst week of his life. He didn't feel safe leaving Mary at home alone. Angela was able to come over a couple of times in order for Don to go to work. However, she had a job and family of her own and couldn't continue to come over all of the time. Don stated that he had called the human resource office at his company to look into whether he could take an early retirement or a leave of absence to care for Mary. Don stated that his company was being terrific about everything. For now they were willing to let him use his vacation and sick time, which he had a great deal of, as needed. His boss was going to look into finding some way for Don to work part-time out of his house if he needed to do that.

At this point Don began crying again.

If this past week is any indication of what it's going to be like in the future, I don't think I'll be able to do it. I'm exhausted. Mary needs me 24 hours a day. She isn't sleeping much at night. Sometimes I'll wake up and hear her pacing and talking to herself. The other night I got out of bed to see what she was doing at 3:30 a.m. She was sitting in her chair looking out the darkened window. She had left the stove on after boiling water for tea. I put her back to bed, and she fell asleep. I couldn't get back to sleep because I was too frightened by the thought of what could have happened if I hadn't checked on her.

The really sad part of all of this is that she has really good days. Like on Tuesday. I woke up and walked into the kitchen. Mary had made coffee and eggs. She smiled at me and said, "Morning, honey. I love you." I thought she was better. In fact, she and I spent the good part of an hour talking about our first date. Mary was able to remember details that I had forgotten. It was wonderful. I decided it was safe to go to work for a while since she was doing so well. When I got home later that day, Mary was back in her chair mumbling to herself and wringing her hands together. She didn't even seem to know I was there. Which I guess was good because I was devastated, and I'm sure if she had really looked at me she would have seen how scared and sad I was.

As I look back on this, I guess it has been building for a long time. When we first went to see Mary's doctor and he began doing all of those tests it was 2 years ago. We've been seeing you for over a year. I remember Mary telling me that she had been forgetting stuff for a while before we went to the doctor. She used to laugh about being so scatter-brained. I know Mary was trying to help her memory for a while before seeing the doctor. I remember seeing those little yellow sticky notes all over the place—"don't forget eggs"—"Andrew's birthday on Friday." Before all of this, she was so organized. She paid all the bills, remembered to send birthday presents, sent all the cards and notes to people. About a month after we started to come to see you, Dr. Kraus, I found an old beat-up brown paper bag stuffed into a kitchen cabinet. Inside the bag was a whole slew of unopened bills and mail. Mary had just thrown everything into the bag. If I hadn't found it when I did, we probably would have lost phone and electric service. They were sending overdue notices! From that time on, I made arrangements to pay the bills. I remember trying to explain to Mary why I decided to do this. She was really hurt.

At that time she still had more good days than bad days. She had always taken great pride in being in charge of the money. I compromised and left her in charge of grocery money, newspaper money, things like that. But after a few months she didn't do anything with her account and I began taking care of everything. Mary never said another word.

I don't think Andrew knows how bad his mother is right now. Angela knows, but we haven't really talked about it. I guess I always just kind of believed that if we never acknowledged it, it wouldn't be true. Andrew's planning on bringing his family out for their usual visit in a couple of weeks. I guess I'd better call him and give him a head's up on just how different his mother will seem to him now. How am I going to tell him?

At this point, Don quietly cried and stared at the floor. Dr. Kraus asked if Don felt it might be helpful to have a session with the children and Don. Don liked this idea, and a session was scheduled during the time that Andrew was going to be in town. Dr. Kraus had given Don the phone numbers of some support groups for families and spouses of Alzheimer's patients. Dr. Kraus encouraged Don to attend a meeting and talk to other people who were going through some of the same things he was going through. Don said he'd see if he could make the time.

You know, Dr. Kraus, I think that until this past week I never really thought that what was happening to Mary was Alzheimer's disease. I thought that she would get better. You know, it came on so slowly. She started getting forgetful years ago, and it just gradually got worse. And it was like God was teasing us, because sometimes she would be really good, like in the old days—we could sit around and talk about all the fun we had and she'd remember everything. She'd laugh and talk. Only this time there's something different about her. She's not really coming back out of it. It's like little pieces of her have died and slowly nothing will be left but a shell. For the first time I'm realizing that I'm losing her for good—we'll never share all the plans we had made for retirement. She'll never see the grandbabies grow up. And worse, they'll never remember what a fantastic lady Mary was . . . is. . . .

Dr. Kraus continued counseling with Don. Don also attended some support groups for families with Alzheimer's, where he received a great deal of support and information. Dr. Kraus no longer met with Mary on a regular basis. It was extremely traumatic for Mary to leave the house, and she stopped being able to communicate in a meaningful way.

Don, Angela, and Andrew tried to keep Mary at home and do the caretaking themselves. This plan worked for about another 5 or 6 months. After that, Mary stopped being able to communicate with them and her aggressive episodes had increased to such a degree that they could not control her behavior. At that point, they discussed their options.

Fortunately, Don and Mary could afford long-term residential health care coverage. Most insurance policies do not cover residential care for Alzheimer's patients. If a person needs to be in a facility that offers 24-hour care, but is not suffering from a medical problem requiring hospitalization, he or she must pay for the residential care themselves. This usually costs thousands of dollars a month. Medicaid coverage will pay for long-term residential care only after a person is declared indigent, which means the person cannot have more than a few thousand dollars. If the person is married, the spouse will also need to be indigent to be eligible for this coverage.

Don wanted to keep Mary at home for as long as possible. He felt that he could have her at home if the insurance company would pay to have aides come during the day and feed and watch Mary. This arrangement would have been much less expensive for the insurance company, but since it was not written in the policy as an option, Don's only alternative was to place Mary in a long-term residential facility.

By the time Mary went to live in the residential facility, she no longer remembered who her children were and was only rarely able to identify Don. She had lost her ability to speak coherently and was required to use a wheelchair. She needed the wheelchair because she had lost her ability to keep her balance when she stood up or walked. The doctors were afraid that she would fall and break a bone if she continued to walk. By the last few months of Mary's life, she was unable to feed herself and required feeding tubes. She had also become incontinent.

For the entire time Mary was in the residential facility, Don visited every day. He sat in her room with her and talked to her about work and the children. He washed and brushed her hair. Angela and Andrew visited often even though Mary did not recognize them and was unable to communicate with them. At the time of Mary's death, Don, Angela, and Andrew were at her bedside.

1. Early-onset Alzheimer's disease is much rarer than late-onset Alzheimer's disease. While it occurs less often, the disease progresses at a much more rapid pace. As scientists continue to research the cause of Alzheimer's disease, they are exploring possible genetic markers for early-onset Alzheimer's. If scientists developed a test to identify with a 100-percent certainty whether or not a person will develop early-onset Alzheimer's, would you take it and want to know the results? Why or why not?

2. Knowing there is no cure for Alzheimer's, what would you do if you discovered that you had this disease?

3. If you were a parent of children aged 5 and 7, would you want to know if they were going to develop this disease? Why or why not?

4. If a medication was developed that would cure this disease, but you had to take the medicine before the onset of any of the symptoms of Alzheimer's disease and there was a 50-percent chance that the cure would kill you, would you take it? Why or why not?

5. If you were a counselor working with Don, Angela, and Andrew, what would you focus on with them?

Name _____ Section _____ Date _____

## ACTIVITY 11-1

This exercise can be done as a class activity, individually, or in small groups.

1. Assume you are a reporter for a newsletter that will be sent to all people aged 65 and older. Write up a list of activities and ways of living that will enhance optimum intellectual and personal functioning for older adults. Base this list on your reading of the textbook and your own personal observations. After each suggestion from the textbook, write whether there has been any research that proves this to be a positive suggestion. After each suggestion based on your own personal observations, write why you believe it will help people.

2. Even though you are not a senior citizen, would you follow the majority of suggestions on your list? Why or why not?

3. At what age should most people begin practicing the suggestions on your list? Why?

4. Are any of your suggestions inappropriate for people of other cultures? Why or why not?

5. Select one of the suggestions based on your own personal observations and design a research study that could prove your premise to be correct. You may use an experimental design, an analogue design, or a qualitative research design. Try to make your study as strong as possible.

Name _____ Section _____ Date _____

# ACTIVITY 11-2

Neuropsychology studies cognition. Neuropsychologists use a variety of methods to assess possible thinking and learning deficits and changes or problems in people's cognitive abilities. Neuropsychological tests are commonly used to assess comprehensive abilities of written and spoken words, mental dexterity, and differences between left- and right-hemisphere dominance, among other things. The Luria-Nebraska and Halstead-Reitan tests are probably two of the most commonly used neuropsychological test batteries.

Trailmaking is an example of one of the subtests used in neuropsychological testing. It helps to examine mental dexterity and the ability to shift between categories. Below and on the following pages are examples of a trailmaking subtest. These examples are used to help you experience what a neuropsychological test might feel like. In no way are these tests to be used as indicators of cognitive abilities or impairments.

### Directions for Trailmaking Test 1

The instructor should time this exercise, or students should be placed into pairs with one timing the other. If students are doing this alone, they should set a timer for themselves.

You will have 90 seconds to complete this exercise. The instructor should read out the time, or one person in the pair should time the other person during this test.

Draw a line connecting the circles in numerical order (1 to 2 to 3, and so on). Do not lift your pencil from the paper while doing this exercise.

Stop when you are done.

Write down the amount of time it took you to finish this test.

If you are in a pair, reverse roles and complete this part of the exercise.

### Directions for Trailmaking Test 2

The instructor should time this exercise, or students should be placed into pairs with one timing the other. If students are doing this alone, they should set a timer for themselves.

You will have 90 seconds to complete this exercise. The instructor should read out the time, or one person in the pair should time the other person during this test.

Draw a line connecting first a number, then a letter, then a number, then a letter, in order (1 to A to 2 to B to 3 to C, and so on). Do not lift your pencil from the paper while doing this exercise.

Stop when you are done.

Write down the amount of time it took you to finish this test.

If you are in a pair, reverse roles and complete this part of the exercise.

**Trailmaking 1**

**Trailmaking 2**

④  Ⓐ
        Ⓒ

    Ⓔ

Ⓖ
            ⑦

⑥      ③  ⑤

            ①

        Ⓕ

②

            Ⓑ
    Ⓓ

1. What differences did you notice in your scores?

2. What do you think caused these differences?

3. Suppose you saved these scores, took this same test 40 years later, and discovered that your new scores were triple what your original scores had been. What are some hypotheses that might explain these differences?

Name _____ Section _____ Date _____

## ACTIVITY 11-3

Work in pairs or groups of three to complete this exercise. One person will be the subject, and the other person will be the experimenter. The subject will listen and try to remember all the information the experimenter says. Then he or she will be asked a series of questions to test memory and the ability to use the information just learned. It is important to remember that this is a fun, experiential exercise and not a test of intelligence or ability.

The subject will need to leave the room for several minutes if this exercise is being completed with more than two people.

The experimenter needs to complete the following worksheet without letting the subject know what is being written.

**Subjects: Do not read any further.**

**Experimenters: Fill in the blanks.**
Make up a list of five common words:

a.

b.

c.

d.

e.

Now add the specified information to complete this story. Write your answers in the spaces provided.

On _____ [day] at _____ [time], _____ [person's name, no. 1], _____ [person's name, no. 2], and _____ [person's name, no. 3] were going to _____ [destination]. While they were

_____ [mode of transportation], a strange thing happened. Just as they were about to _____ [activity], _____ [person no. 2] yelled, "Stop, look over there!" When they looked over there, they were all amazed to see _____. [Be creative! What did they see?]

_____ [person no. 3] said, "We need to call _____ [pick another person, no. 4] at _____ [phone number with area code]; he [or she] needs to see this. I remember on _____ [pick a date], something similar happened in _____ [pick a place]. A story was written about it in _____ [pick a magazine or newspaper]." Everyone laughed when _____ [person no. 2] said that maybe they all would become famous.

_____ [person no. 1] said that he [or she] didn't want to be famous.

_____ [person no. 2] said that he [or she] would love to be famous because people would give him [or her] free stuff, he [or she] could get thousands of dates, and, most important, he [or she] would _____ [make up a reason].

Ask the subject to rejoin the group if the subject is outside. Have the subject sit comfortably in a chair, with the experimenter sitting across from them.

Experimenter: Say "I am going to give you a list of five words that I want you to remember." Then read the list you developed at the beginning of the exercise. Read the list slowly, allowing the subject about 3 to 5 seconds between words. Experimenter: Say "Now I am going to tell you a short story. I want you to listen carefully and to concentrate. At the end of the story I am going to ask you questions about what I just told you. This is a test of your memory and concentration." Slowly read your story. After you finish reading the story, ask the subject the following questions. Write down his or her answers.

1. What was the area code and phone number that they called?

2. Where were they going?

3. Who said he or she didn't want to be famous?

4. What day was it?

5. What was the name of the magazine or newspaper mentioned in the story?

6. What were the names of the three people in the beginning of the story?

7. What did they see?

8. Who wanted to be famous?

9. What were the three reasons that person wanted to be famous?

10. What were the five words you were asked to remember at the beginning of the exercise?

    a.

    b.

    c.

    d.

    e.

Spend a few minutes talking about the exercise.

11. What general observations did all of you make about memory and concentration?

**Subjects:**
12. Describe how this exercise was for you. How did it make you feel?

13. What sort of things were the easiest for you to remember? Why?

14. What sort of things were the most difficult for you to remember? Why?

15. Did you use any tricks or tools to help you remember certain information? What were they?

16. Imagine yourself in 50 or 60 years. You are beginning to have trouble remembering new information. How do you think you might feel?

17. If you knew that you would never regain your ability to remember or to learn new information, how might you feel? What would you do?

**Experimenter:**
18. What feelings did you notice the subject experiencing as you were telling the story?

19. What feelings did you notice the subject experiencing while you were asking the questions?

20. How did you feel as you were completing this exercise?

21. Imagine yourself in 50 or 60 years. You are beginning to have trouble remembering new information. How do you think you might feel?

22. If you knew that you would never regain your ability to remember or to learn new information, how might you feel? What would you do?

Name _____ Section _____ Date _____

## ACTIVITY 11-4

Many cognitive disorders and impairments are caused by head injuries. The cost of treating, rehabilitating, and caring for people with head injuries resulting from accidents is tremendous. In order to protect people from head injuries, many states have passed mandatory helmet laws for motorcycle riders.

1. What are the pros and cons of mandatory helmet laws?

2. If after one violation or warning, a person chooses to ignore the mandatory helmet law and then sustains a massive head injury, who should be responsible for the thousands of dollars it will cost to care for the person for the rest of their life? Should it be the individual, the insurance companies, the family, or taxpayers? Explain your answer.

3. What would you do if this person did not have insurance or money?

4. What would you do if this person was 16 years old at the time of the accident and would need care for another 60 years?

5. Considering the enormous cost of what could be preventable head injuries, do you believe we should institute mandatory helmet laws for bicyclists, skateboarders, and inline skaters? Why or why not?

Name _____ Section _____ Date _____

## ACTIVITY 11-5

Fetal alcohol syndrome is the single largest preventable cause of mental retardation in the United States. Warning labels are now required on alcoholic beverages and in bars, restaurants, and grocery stores. The problem continues. In small groups, brainstorm solutions to the problem of fetal alcohol syndrome. Explore prevention, intervention, and treatment options for this problem. Discuss possible cultural biases and influences that might affect your solution. Be creative in your problem solving. See if you can come up with some really wild ideas that may not have been explored. Use the following outline if it will help you.

1. What are the causes of pregnant women drinking (explore these from a personal level, a sociocultural level, a corporate level, and a global level)?

2. What influences a pregnant woman to continue drinking? What influences decrease the likelihood that a pregnant woman will seek help to stop drinking?

3. What barriers exist to treatment for alcoholism?

4. What cultural responses discourage intervention for women who continue to drink while pregnant?

5. What are possible solutions to these problems?

6. What are possible obstacles to your solutions?

# CHAPTER 12

# DISORDERS OF CHILDHOOD AND ADOLESCENCE

## ATTENTION-DEFICIT/HYPERACTIVITY DISORDER

Charlie is a 6-year-old boy who has been referred to Dr. Murray for evaluation for possible attention-deficit/hyperactivity disorder. His parents brought him in to see Dr. Murray on the recommendation of his school and pediatrician. Charlie has been suspended from school until a solution for his disruptive behavior can be found. Charlie, his parents, and his younger sister have all come in to see Dr. Murray.

## PERSONAL HISTORY

Charlie is a thin, pale, 6-year-old White male who has unruly blond hair and blue eyes. He arrived at the session wearing a dirty, striped T-shirt; cutoff jean shorts; and worn-out high-top sneakers. When the family was shown into Dr. Murray's office, Charlie's mother kept apologizing for Charlie's appearance, stating that he starts off clean and neat in the morning, but within 10 minutes he looks like a "ragamuffin."

Charlie raced into Dr. Murray's office, slowing down just long enough to discover a corner filled with toys and games. He let out an excited yell and grabbed one of the model airplanes, proceeding to run around the office making airplane noises. His mother tried to grab his arm and told him to put the plane down and sit nicely. Charlie shook off her hand and ignored her request, running to the corner to grab a different toy. He then started playing with some plastic action figures, making them shoot at and kill each other. He smashed the figures into each other loudly. Charlie's mother ran over and took the toys out of Charlie's hands and told him to sit down. Charlie smiled and grabbed a plastic puzzle cube and proceeded to play with that.

Charlie's father had been sitting quietly, ignoring what was happening. He finally got out of his chair and grabbed the puzzle and grabbed Charlie by the arm and sat him down on the couch. "Listen to your mother, Charlie. I'm sick and tired of having to make you listen. Do you hear me? Do you?" Charlie appeared to pout for about 2 minutes. Then he asked Dr. Murray in a loud voice about the telephone on his desk. Charlie tried to get up to touch the phone, but his father grabbed him and held him in his seat. Charlie then noticed a large stuffed bear on the shelf and asked if he could please play with the bear. His mother got the bear and gave it to Charlie. His father continued to hold him in his seat. Charlie threw the bear in the air and caught it. As he was trying to throw it in the air again, his father grabbed the bear and put it on the floor. Charlie then began to play with his tennis shoe, pulling at a loose piece of rubber on the side. Within a minute he had ripped his shoe open. He then stuck his finger in the hole he had made and tried to make it bigger. His father grabbed Charlie's hand and held it so Charlie could not move.

During all of this, Charlie's younger sister had found some crayons and a coloring book and was sitting on the floor in a corner coloring. Charlie begged his father to let him go color with his sister. Charlie's father looked Charlie in the eye and told him that he had to sit quietly and color and that if he did not, he would have to return to sit on the couch again. Charlie promised. He ran over to where his sister was coloring and grabbed her coloring book and crayons. His father immediately grabbed Charlie and returned him to the couch. Charlie was howling that he just wanted to color. He then started to cry loudly.

Dr. Murray told Charlie's parents that he had a kids' room next door. It was equipped with toys and games and was soundproof, but they would be able to watch Charlie through the two-way mirror. Dr. Murray showed Charlie the special kids' room and asked him if he wanted to play in it. Charlie stopped crying and excitedly yelled, "Yeah!" Dr. Murray took Charlie to the room and then returned to ask his sister if she would like to go there, too. At first she was reluctant to go into the room with Charlie, but Dr. Murray thought it very important that he be able to talk openly and honestly with Charlie's parents and felt it was inappropriate for Charlie's sister to remain in the room. After her mother coaxed her and convinced her to go into the room, the three adults sat down in Dr. Murray's office to talk.

Charlie's father sank down into the couch and threw up his hands. "Do you see what we have to put up with? He's like this 24 hours a day! It's like we don't know what to do with him anymore. There are times when I almost wish we could cage him up for 30 minutes just to get a rest. The school is fed up with him, too."

Charlie's mother began to cry softly. "He can be very sweet. He is very compassionate. He just can't seem to control himself. Nothing we do works. We've tried bribing him, punishing him, ignoring him, giving him 'time out'

. . . nothing has made any difference. The school has tried and tried with Charlie. They say he is bright, but that his behaviors are so bad that he is failing and causing such severe disruptions that other children are not able to learn when Charlie is at school. I don't blame them for kicking him out. It's really not fair to the other children. But, what about what's fair for Charlie?"

Dr. Murray told Charlie's parents that he had reviewed the assessment tests the school had completed on Charlie, read the report of Charlie's pediatrician, and interviewed Charlie's teachers. Dr. Murray felt that Charlie was exhibiting symptoms of attention-deficit/hyperactivity disorder. "What this means is that Charlie has problems sustaining attention, does not seem to listen when he is being spoken to, is careless in following through with work, has problems organizing his tasks and activities, is easily distracted by the things going on around him, often forgets what he is supposed to be doing, can't seem to sit still, runs around inappropriately, cannot play quietly by himself, and interrupts others."

Charlie's parents were amazed that Dr. Murray was able to so accurately describe Charlie's behavior. Charlie's father asked why Charlie was the way he was. He said, "Charlie is so different from me, his mom, and his sister. Why is he like this?" Dr. Murray explained that no one fully understands what causes attention-deficit/hyperactivity disorder. The research has indicated that this disorder may run in families. Charlie's father said he had a younger brother who was sort of like Charlie. His brother had always had problems in school and had trouble holding down a job when he was younger. His brother dropped out of high school, "kicked around for a while doing odd jobs, and getting into trouble. Finally he enlisted in the Marines. It seemed to do him a lot of good. When he came out of the Marines, he had learned helicopter maintenance and continued to work fixing helicopters. He still has trouble sitting still, but as long as he can work with his hands and doesn't have to do paperwork, he does okay."

Dr. Murray said that he'd like to try giving Ritalin (methylphenidate) to Charlie. He explained that Ritalin was a stimulant, but seemed to have what was called a paradoxical effect on people with ADHD, whom it calmed. Dr. Murray explained that there were side effects that some children developed when they took Ritalin. These side effects included irritability, sleeplessness, loss of appetite, and growth retardation.

Dr. Murray explained to Charlie's parents that he strongly believed that Charlie would also need to be in therapy to learn to control his behavior and to learn appropriate socialization skills. The Ritalin was a tool to allow Charlie to be able to focus on learning how to control his behavior and to allow him to attend school. Dr. Murray strongly felt that children should not be kept on Ritalin for years and years and thus needed to learn how to control their behaviors without the drug. Dr. Murray suggested that Charlie's assessment tests indicated he may also have a mild learning disability and that he would like to work with the school on a special education program that focused on remediating this disability so Charlie could learn to learn. Dr. Murray further explained that it would be important that the behavioral programs also be implemented in the home as well as at school. Charlie would need consistency. Behaviors that are unacceptable at school must also be unacceptable at home.

After Charlie learned new behaviors and would follow through with his programs at home and at school, Dr. Murray wanted to start Charlie in a social skills group with other children his age. Because of his ADHD Charlie had not been able to develop any friendships—other children did not want to play with him because he could not wait his turn or would not follow the rules, or simply because his behavior was just odd. Dr. Murray ran a group for children to help them learn how to interact, listen, and communicate.

Dr. Murray also recommended that Charlie's parents attend a parenting group he ran specifically for parents of children with ADHD. Children with ADHD require some specialized parenting skills—they need to learn how to set up and enforce a strict behavioral program, they need to be educated about appropriate expectations, and they benefit from the support of other parents who are experiencing a lot of the same stresses they have in raising an ADHD child.

1. There is a large controversy concerning the overdiagnosis and treatment of ADHD. Many critics claim that normal children are being put on Ritalin in order to control the normal boisterous behaviors involved with being a child. Do you think ADHD is being overdiagnosed and treated? Why or why not?

2. What things within today's culture might contribute to the increased incidence of ADHD in children?

3. How might a diagnosis of ADHD affect a child's sense of self-efficacy and self-esteem?

**EATING DISORDER**

Mary, a 32-year-old White female university student, came to the health center at the university. She stated that she was feeling very depressed and anxious all of the time and wanted to get some medication to help her get through life. She said that she was not interested in any counseling; she just wanted some prescriptions. The policy of the university health center was not to prescribe any medications for psychological conditions without individual counseling. Reluctantly, Mary agreed to see a counselor as long as she also was given a prescription for an antidepressant and an antianxiety medication.

Mary's case was assigned to Kathleen, one of the interns working at the counseling center. Kathleen was finishing her master's degree in counseling and was completing her internship by working at the counseling center.

Mary showed up for her first session 20 minutes late. She said she had gotten caught up in something and had lost track of time. When Mary had first come to the health center requesting a prescription, she had been given a lengthy intake packet to complete before her first counseling session. When Kathleen asked about the packet, Mary said she must have left it at home. She asked Kathleen whether she could just take another one home and bring it in next time. Kathleen said no, they would need to spend the rest of this session filling out the packet together. Mary seemed put out by this answer, but went along with Kathleen. After the first two questions, Mary interrupted Kathleen and asked when she could get her prescription. "You know, I don't think I really will benefit from this counseling at all. I know all I need is a little medication to help me through this tough time. I don't really like talking about myself and my problems. Is this all really necessary?" Kathleen assured her that it was necessary, and it was policy. She further stated that at each session she would give Mary her pills for the next week. Mary said that the protocol felt childish and demeaning. Kathleen assured her that it was standard operating procedure for new clients and that once they had been working together for a while this protocol could be changed. This was not actually standard procedure for all new clients, but it was the policy for suicidal or high-risk clients. Kathleen felt that if Mary were given a full prescription she would not comply with the counseling. It was Kathleen's intention to evaluate where Mary was in terms of her investment in the counseling before changing the protocol.

As the first session came to a close, it was obvious that Mary was depressed and anxious. However, there seemed to be something more going on with Mary than she was willing to talk about during this first session. By the end of the session, Mary seemed to have reluctantly begun to trust Kathleen and was willing to make another appointment for the next week.

**PERSONAL HISTORY**

Mary came to her first session wearing old blue jeans, an old faded T-shirt, and old worn-out sneakers. She carried a backpack, water bottle, sweatshirt, umbrella, lunch bag, and purse. She was of average height and slightly overweight. Her hair was dyed a medium blonde, but she had not dyed it in a while, as several inches of dark brown roots showed. Her hair was pulled back in a messy ponytail. She wore no makeup but had a flawless complexion and beautiful blue eyes.

Mary stated that she returned to school this past year in order to finish her degree and then go on for her elementary education teaching certificate. She said that she had been a student at a large, private southern university for 2 years before dropping out and getting married. Mary said she was returning to school because she had recently been divorced and needed to find a job that would pay enough to support her and her two children. She is currently receiving alimony and child support but doesn't trust her ex-husband to continue to "do the right thing." By being able to support herself and her children, Mary would feel more secure.

During the first several counseling sessions with Kathleen, Mary was reluctant to talk about herself. Kathleen spent a great deal of time asking questions and getting minimal or vague answers. Mary finally admitted during the fourth session that she had a very difficult time trusting people. This lack of trust was founded on some very painful experiences. "Hurt me once, shame on you. Hurt me twice, shame on me," she said.

Mary stated that she couldn't remember when the depression set in:

It almost feels like it was there from the time I was a teenager. I remember being a happy kid. I was a bit of a tomboy. I loved playing with my brother (he's 2 years younger than me). We used to have a gang of kids, mostly boys, who we'd run around with all the time. It's not like nowadays—when I was a kid we could run all over the neighborhood and play in the forests and open fields without our parents worrying about some sicko trying to molest us or kidnap us.

We used to make forts and have clubs. It was great. Then, when I was about 11, I started to develop physically. It was terrible. I have a vivid memory of my brother and our friends noticing I was growing hair under my arms and making fun of me. I remember I stopped playing with them when I was 12—I remember because that's when I started developing breasts. I could no longer be one of the gang. I was really kind of sad.

My mom tried to get me interested in other things—cooking, Girl Scouts, sewing. That was all okay. I do remember gaining a lot of weight. I was always sort of average. I ran around a lot with my gang of friends; doing that, I think, burned off excess fat really easily. When I stopped running around so much and became more of a girl, I found I gained weight. I wasn't fat or anything as I look back on it now. It's weird, when I look at old picture of myself in junior high and high school I see a pretty girl who wasn't even plump. But I remember feeling really fat back then. I remember my dad calling me "butterball" from the time I was a baby. I don't think he meant it as a reference to my weight, but as I grew older I took it that way. Each time he'd say it as an endearment, I'd cross my arms in front of my stomach and try to look skinny.

By the time I was in seventh or eighth grade I remember being glad I was a girl. I had some best girlfriends, and we would have slumber parties every weekend. We would spend the evenings putting on Miss America pageants, parading around in our nightgowns and doing talent contests. And we would dance, listen to records, talk about boys, and eat junk food. It was so much fun to just sit and laugh and eat Ding-Dongs, potato chips, pizza, and ice cream. We would stay up all night laughing and eating and carrying on—it was great.

When I started high school there was this unbelievable pressure to be beautiful. In the South, where I grew up, all little girls were primed from an early age to be homecoming queen or a cheerleader. I was never really good at gymnastics, and I was pretty insecure, so I never even tried out for cheerleading. I figured I was too fat and ugly and uncoordinated to be a cheerleader. Which is really kind of sad, because as I look back on my old pictures I see a very pretty young girl who was not ugly or fat. And in reality I was pretty athletic and probably could have made a good cheerleader. I remember looking at magazines when I was in high school and wishing I could be those girls. They never had a bad hair day, or pimples, or fat.

My momma was one of those Southern belles. She was gracious and beautiful—in fact, she still is. She really was like Beaver Cleaver's mother, June. She wore dresses and pearls and heels to go grocery shopping. In fact, she still does. I remember the first time I saw her wearing jeans—it was like 5 years ago—I thought it was so funny I couldn't stop laughing! She actually looked really good in them; it was just the concept of *my* mother wearing jeans that set me off. My mother has soft blond hair that is, of course, naturally wavy. She has my eyes. And she is naturally skinny. She eats a lot, but you'd never know it to look at her. She has a real sweet tooth and is always eating cakes, pies, doughnuts, cookies, and candy. All day long she eats sweets and never gains a pound. She doesn't work out or jog or anything! I'm so envious of her. Of course, my brother inherited her metabolism. He's skinny as a rail and eats like a horse. I inherited my father's metabolism. He's rather chunky and gains weight in a second. He plays handball five times a week and golfs on weekends.

It was tough growing up around my house. I always felt like I could never compare with my mother beauty-wise. My brother was naturally athletic and outgoing. He was always Mr. Popularity. Everybody always loved my dad. He's just the nicest man in the world. And then there was me. I felt like a plain Jane—just average, nobody special. I know my parents loved me; I even know my brother loved me. I just didn't love me. My family never, ever put me down or anything. In fact, I would describe my family as extremely close. I still talk to my parents every day. My brother and his family and me and my family all spend Christmas holidays with my parents. We all vacation in the summers together at our family lake house. I think that my family might have been one of the reasons my ex-husband wanted to marry me, and later they might have been one of the reasons he wanted to divorce me.

I love my parents so much. I would absolutely die if anything happened to them. It's kind of embarrassing to admit, but I don't think I ever made a big decision without first talking everything over with them. The only time I didn't take their advice was when I married Jim. They thought we were too young to get married. I was 20, and Jim was 22. We had been going out for about 6 months when we got engaged. We got married about a month later. After we got engaged and married, my family was always very supportive of us. They never gave us grief over our decision to marry. In fact, they never once said "I told you so" to me when I was getting divorced. They just would never do something like that.

Jim was an only child of a single mother. I think he was really lonely and isolated. He once told me that the way he survived his childhood was to get sort of adopted into the families of his friends. Jim is a really charming and funny guy. He had a way of endearing himself to everyone around him. My parents were always really kind to Jim. They are kind to everyone. But my dad and mom would call him Son, and he would call them Mom and Dad. I know that Jim's philandering and lying hurt my parents a lot.

My mom and I have a very special relationship. We can read each other's minds. My mom can tell when something is bothering me, and she seems to know just what to say to make me feel better. I'm sometimes not very good with words. My mom can put my thoughts and feelings into words better than I can. She is my best friend in the world. In fact, I am thinking of taking my girls back home to live with my parents while I go to school. My parents would love to have all of us living with them. I would love to be close to them again. The reason I'm living here now is because Jim got a job and we bought a house. As part of the divorce settlement I got the house. If I decide to move I'll have to go through the hassle of selling the house and claiming capital gains tax on the money. And Jim has threatened to sue for custody if I try to move the girls out of state. My parents said they would pay for a lawyer to fight for custody if I moved back home. I really don't want to have to put the girls through any more ugly divorce stuff. But I really think I need my family.

This drives Jim nuts. By the end of our marriage he was accusing my parents of coming between us. He said I couldn't make a decision without them and didn't have a thought in my empty head that they didn't put there. I was really hurt and angry. I know I talk to them a lot, but I really value their advice. They are wise and kind people.

At this point Mary broke down into tears. She said that the worst thing was that she was feeling caught between a rock and a hard place. She grabbed a pillow off of the couch and curled her body around it in a fetal position and whimpered. When she finally calmed herself enough to continue talking she sounded like a little girl.

I haven't told you the whole story. I am just so ashamed. I don't know what to do about it. I guess I'll just tell you. [Mary wouldn't even look at Kathleen when she was talking. She was still curled around the pillow and speaking very softly.] I am sick. I know I have a problem. I binge on junk food—really, really bad food—and then I make myself vomit, and I take laxatives. I'm just so ashamed. Jim is the only one who knows about this—and he only knows because he caught me doing it one time. He got me to confess to him that I had been doing this since I was 16 years old. By the time he caught me 2 years ago I had been doing it for 14 years. I think my old dentist knew. He told me that my back teeth were rotting away and asked me point-blank if I had bulimia. I was shocked and scared and told him no, that my whole family had weak enamel. I don't think he believed me, but he didn't pursue it. I never went back to see him again.

After Jim found out, he tried to get me to stop. I really wanted to stop doing this. He tried helping me in a lot of different ways. He begged me to go to counseling. I was too ashamed to go. He tried bribing me with vacations, money, even jewelry—but nothing worked. Then he tried shaming me into stopping by calling me a human garbage dump and ridiculing me. That didn't work because I would just cry and agree with him. By the end of our marriage he was so disgusted with me that he said he had those affairs with other women because I made him sick to his stomach, and there was no way he could love a pile of garbage like me.

You know the sad thing . . . all those hurtful things he said to me only reinforced my own beliefs about myself. I thought I was a hundred times worse than anything Jim could ever think of calling me. I disgusted myself worse than I could ever disgust anyone else. The worse our marriage got the more I binged and purged. By the end of the marriage I was doing it daily. Now I am still doing it four or five times a week. The only reason I don't do it more is because the girls are old enough to stay awake later and I can't be alone, and I won't do it when they are awake. I do it all day long when they are with their dad for the weekend. It's really, really sick. It feels totally out of control. Which is a really weird thing, because I think the reason I started doing it in the first place was to get some control.

I guess now that you know my deep dark secret you'll not want anything to do with me.

Kathleen assured her that she would not want to stop working with her; in fact, she thought that what Mary just did was incredibly brave. Kathleen told Mary that by telling her this she had taken the most important step in beginning her healing.

In order for Kathleen to begin treating Mary's bulimia, she needed to get an accurate sense of the severity of her disorder. Although Mary was very ashamed and embarrassed by her bingeing behavior, she was honest with Kathleen. Mary confessed to eating just about anything that was in the house, as long as it was a lot of food. She preferred bingeing on the same types of food she remembers eating at the slumber parties she attended as a teen—cookies, pizza, candy, chips. She also had specific bingeing foods she used when she was feeling particularly sad—these were usually foods she associated with her mother, such as pies, cakes, doughnuts. But Mary confessed to eating entire boxes of cereal or loaves of toast or jars of peanut butter if there was nothing else in the house to eat. On the weekends when the girls were with Jim, Mary would eat the most. She said it was because she was so lonely and upset. She also admitted it was because she was able to do it all day long and eat anything she wanted to eat. She would binge on huge buckets of fried chicken, mashed potatoes and gravy, and biscuits—things she would never allow her girls to eat. "I want to fill up that empty hole inside of me, and food seems to do the trick. Except I get terrified of getting fat, and then I puke."

Mary talked about getting fat as if it is something worse than cancer or death. She said that where she grew up, it was the worst thing that a girl could do.

It was interesting growing up in a culture where beauty and grace are so highly valued. The strange thing was that in order to really be seen as beautiful and gracious, everything had to appear effortless. You would never see women jogging or lifting weights. Women are either beautiful or not. No one who is truly beautiful has to diet or would ever gain weight. As strange as that sounds—that's my mother! That's all the girls I was in sorority with and all the girls I grew up with. They could all eat anything they wanted and still remain thin. They never dieted or exercised. They just were beautiful.

Mary talked about bingeing and purging as a way to be beautiful and not appear to diet. She was also addicted to laxatives. She had taken laxatives for so many years that she was sure her body could not properly eliminate waste without them. She tried to give laxatives up about 5 years before when she found blood in her stool, became frightened, and stopped using them for about 2 weeks. During those 2 weeks she was miserable. She became constipated, and she imagined gaining lots and lots of weight during that time. Finally she gave in and began using laxatives again. Now she has weaned herself to using them only on the days that she binges.

Mary said her bulimia is the only secret she has ever kept from her mother because it is just too shameful. She thought that her mother might suspect there is something going on but doesn't know that it's bulimia. "My parents have always been just so proud of me. I have tried to be perfect for them. This would devastate them." As she talked more, she confessed that a major reason she didn't immediately pack up the girls and move back home with her parents was that she could not continue to binge and purge when living under the same roof as her mother. Mary desperately wanted to move back home, but couldn't give up bingeing and purging.

1. Freud believed that eating disorders were manifestations of unconscious conflicts. If you assume this to be true, what unconscious conflicts can you hypothesize Mary might be battling with?

2. Behavioral psychologists believe that conditioning plays the major role in the development of eating disorders. They presume food avoidance or overindulgence is somehow reinforced. Looking at Mary's life, what evidence could you find that might support this hypothesis?

3. Family systems therapists believe that families with members who have eating disorders are enmeshed. That means roles are blurred, and family members are too overprotective or involved in one another's lives, to the point that individuality and autonomy are lost. What evidence do you find in Mary's story to support this hypothesis?

4. Social psychologists believe that eating disorders develop because of cultural standards for beauty. What evidence do you find in Mary's story to support this hypothesis?

5. After examining all of these theories, what do you think is the cause of Mary's eating disorder?

After the treatment team at the counseling center—the psychiatrists, staff psychologists, a nutritionist, and a nurse-practitioner—discussed Mary's case, it was decided that the best treatment would be a combination of antidepressant medication, nutritional education, response-prevention therapy, and cognitive-behavioral therapy. Mary had responded well to Prozac, so it was decided that she should continue to take it while proceeding with the rest of her therapy. Mary had a long history of rigid thinking about food. She categorized food as being good or bad. When she was not bingeing, Mary was very strict about what and how much she allowed herself to eat. When Mary began working with the nutritionist, it was discovered that when Mary was not bingeing she limited herself to about 600 calories a day. This rigid, near-starvation diet was believed to be a large part of what triggered Mary's need to binge. Mary and the nutritionist worked out a sensible 1,200-to-1,500-calorie-a-day diet that gradually began to include foods that Mary had always labeled as bad. It was important that Mary learn that food was neither good nor bad and that eating or not did not make her good or bad. After Mary followed her diet for a few months and began to control her bingeing and purging, a response-prevention program was used to help her learn to stop the purging associated with certain foods she considered bad. In conjunction with these therapies, Kathleen continued to work with Mary on her cognitive distortions concerning weight and appearance. They worked on replacing Mary's distorted beliefs about her weight with more adaptive beliefs. They also worked on Mary's enmeshment with her family, particularly her mother.

As Mary began to feel more in control over her bulimia, her sense of herself as a strong individual grew. She was able to confront her cognitive distortions about being damaged, dirty, and garbage. She began to feel stronger and more secure in who she was. Mary continued treatment for 2 years; at the end of that time, she had not binged and purged for over 8 months. She was also completing her teaching certificate and had started a new relationship with a man who knew about her bulimia and was loving and supportive of her continued growth. Mary knew that she would need to continue to fight off occasional urges to binge and purge, but she also knew that she was strong enough to win these fights.

6. From a sociocultural point of view, what message do you think we send young women about looks and weight?

7. What messages does our culture send young men about their looks and weight?

8. List some examples of movie and television characters, entertainers, athletes, and other celebrities who seem to be the role models for appearance and weight for young people today.

9. How many of these examples do you think are healthy role models?

10. What do you think we can do to help change the negative sociocultural influences that affect young girls and boys to the extent that they develop eating disorders?

Name _____ Section _____ Date _____

## ACTIVITY 12-1

**Vignette 1**

David is a 7-year-old White boy whose parents have brought him in for counseling. As David sat sullenly on the couch next to his mother, David's father began by telling the counselor how embarrassing it was to be there and how he couldn't believe how stubborn his son was. David's father was obviously getting angry as he began to talk, and David's mother interrupted to softly explain that David had a little problem. David obviously became uncomfortable as the discussion continued, and when he began to bang his foot against the couch, his father immediately yelled at him to stop. David's mother said that David's little problem was that he seemed to have trouble with "elimination." When she was asked to explain what that meant, David's father broke in and said his son "craps his pants like a baby in a diaper." David has been to many medical doctors to see if there is a physical reason for this problem. None of them could find a reason, and they recommended counseling. Apparently David began having problems 2 years ago, when he started school. His mother reported that before that time David had been fully toilet trained. David has accidents about three times a week.

1. What *DSM-IV* diagnosis would you assign to David?

    a. Axis I:

    b. Axis II:

    c. Axis III:

    d. Axis IV:

    e. Axis V:

2. On what criteria do you base your diagnosis?

**Vignette 2**

You are a counselor at a junior high school. Travis was referred to you, again, because he was in another fight. Travis has a long history of fighting and bullying other children. He typically only fights kids who are younger and much smaller. This is the third fight he has been in in the past 2 months. For the first time, Travis used a knife. As a result, the school is going to suspend Travis for at least a month. Travis is the youngest son of a single mother. His older brother is in juvenile detention for attempted rape. Travis's mother works long hours and admits that she isn't home enough. Travis has been in trouble with the police in the past for breaking the windows on a new house being built in his neighborhood and for stealing from some younger children. The school is requiring that Travis and his mother get counseling before they will allow Travis to return to school.

3. What *DSM-IV* diagnosis would you assign to Travis?

   a. Axis I:

   b. Axis II:

   c. Axis III:

   d. Axis IV:

   e. Axis V:

4. On what criteria do you base your diagnosis?

184 CHAPTER 12 / DISORDERS OF CHILDHOOD AND ADOLESCENCE

**Vignette 3**

Amanda is an 11-year-old girl who, along with her parents, was referred to you for counseling. Amanda's parents and her school are very concerned about Amanda's behavior. She has no friends at school or at home. No one will play with her because she is angry and hostile. She cannot play any games because the minute it looks as if she is not winning she throws a tantrum and refuses to continue. Her parents are frustrated because Amanda ignores their requests or tells them "no." They feel angry, resentful, and impotent. When Amanda is confronted with something she has done wrong, she refuses to listen or accept responsibility for it. Instead, she blames everyone and everything else. Her parents and teachers cannot talk to Amanda because she immediately becomes angry and hostile.

5. What *DSM-IV* diagnosis would you assign to Amanda?

    a. Axis I:

    b. Axis II:

    c. Axis III:

    d. Axis IV:

    e. Axis V:

6. On what criteria do you base your diagnosis?

**Vignette 4**

Shannon is a beautiful 8-year-old girl who was referred to you for therapy by her medical doctor. About a year ago, Shannon's parents noticed that she would do what they called a grimace—she would bite down hard and scrunch up her face and then quickly jerk her head to the right. This grimacing began to get more and more frequent as the year progressed. A few months ago it had gotten so bad that they took Shannon to her pediatrician because they were afraid she had a brain tumor or something. About that time, Shannon began making a strange grunting sound. This grunting would happen at different times of the day. At first her parents punished Shannon, trying to get her to stop grunting. Shannon would cry and cry, but never seemed to be able to stop. Shannon has been having a lot of trouble at school because the other children are cruel to her. Shannon's pediatrician could find no medical explanation for Shannon's behavior.

7. What *DSM-IV* diagnosis would you assign to Shannon?

    a. Axis I:

    b. Axis II:

    c. Axis III:

    d. Axis IV:

    e. Axis V:

8. On what criteria do you base your diagnosis?

**Vignette 5**

Joshua is a 4-year-old boy who has been in and out of foster care from the time of his birth. Joshua appears small for his age, but other than that he is within the normal range in all developmental milestones. Joshua's current foster mother brought Joshua in to be evaluated because Joshua makes only limited eye contact with anyone, does not laugh or respond to games of peek-a-boo or tickling, and cries when she leaves the room but then doesn't respond to her when she returns or tries to cuddle him. The case notes for Joshua show that when he was born he was first placed into foster care with an aunt. His aunt was young and developed a drug problem while Joshua was living with her. It was later discovered that his aunt sometimes left Joshua alone in his crib all day. When he was finally taken from his aunt and placed in another situation, Joshua was malnourished and had a serious urinary tract infection as well as a skin disorder on his buttocks caused by having dirty diapers left on him for days.

9. What *DSM-IV* diagnosis would you assign to Joshua?

    a. Axis I:

    b. Axis II:

    c. Axis III:

    d. Axis IV:

    e. Axis V:

10. On what criteria do you base your diagnosis?

**Vignette 6**

Casey is the 4-year-old son of two successful insurance executives. His older sister is 7 years old. Casey's parents brought him in for an evaluation because they have become very concerned over some of his behaviors. Casey's older sister is bright and highly verbal. She reached all of her developmental milestones early. She is very close to Casey. When Casey was younger he was a bright, outgoing, loving young boy. When he was about 2 years old, his behavior began to change. He seemed to retreat into a world of his own. He never played with other children. He would sit for hours running his trucks back and forth in front of him. He lined up his trucks and would become angry if anyone touched or moved them. He never really began talking. At first his parents assumed it was because his sister did all the talking for him—"Casey wants a cookie," or "Casey needs to go to the bathroom," she would say. When his sister was not around, Casey pointed to what he wanted or leaned his body toward what he needed. He never shared his ideas, thoughts, or emotions. Casey still does not speak.

11. What *DSM-IV* diagnosis would you assign to Casey?

   a. Axis I:

   b. Axis II:

   c. Axis III:

   d. Axis IV:

   e. Axis V:

12. On what criteria do you base your diagnosis?

**Vignette 7**

Linda is an 8-year-old girl whose mother has brought her in for therapy. Three months before, Linda started refusing to go to school in the mornings, claiming she was sick. At first her mother allowed Linda to stay home, and she eventually took her to the pediatrician to see what was the matter with Linda. The pediatrician could not find any reason for Linda's stomachaches. During the day, while Linda was home with her mother, her stomachaches would disappear. Linda started having the same stomachaches when her mother would leave to play tennis on the weekends or go out with her father. Linda started following her mother everywhere. She began insisting that her mother sleep with her at night. Her mother refused to do this, but would discover that Linda had snuck into her bedroom during the night and slept on the floor by the bed. As Linda's mother became more insistent that Linda go to school, Linda became more and more afraid, crying incessantly and making herself throw up in the mornings.

13. What *DSM-IV* diagnosis would you assign to Linda?

   a. Axis I:

   b. Axis II:

   c. Axis III:

   d. Axis IV:

   e. Axis V:

14. On what criteria do you base your diagnosis?

Name _____ Section _____ Date _____

## ACTIVITY 12-2

1. For many years it was believed that children did not suffer from anxiety or depression. It was assumed that these were disorders of adulthood that were associated with the pressures of daily living. Do you believe children can be anxious or depressed? Why or why not?

2. Think back to your childhood. List some of the things that could have led you to become either anxious or depressed.

3. Now consider the world that today's children are growing up in. List some of the things that could lead to anxiety or depression today.

4. What are some things in the world today that might significantly impact a teen's sense of well-being?

5. How can we teach children and teens to handle these situations so they do not develop anxiety or depression disorders?

6. What impact, if any, do you think culture has on the development of coping skills in children and adolescents?

7. Do you believe it is possible for us to develop a culture of coping within the current society? Why or why not?

Name _____ Section _____ Date _____

## ACTIVITY 12-3

Childhood mental disorders can be very difficult to diagnose and define due to the variation in abilities and expectations for various age levels. What is seen as normal and appropriate behavior for a 2-year-old—such as wetting the pants—would be seen as a problem for a 12-year-old. After each behavior, write down at what age you would recommend a child for counseling if he or she exhibited the behavior. Assume that the children are all of normal intelligence and that there is nothing physically wrong with them.

1. Defecating in his or her pants three times a week.

2. Not being able to sit still to complete a 30-minute project.

3. Not being able to wait for a turn when playing checkers.

4. Stealing toys from a friend.

5. Pulling the wings off of flies just to see what happens.

6. Crying when a parent leaves him or her at school or someone's house.

7. Throwing temper tantrums when asked to clean up his or her room three times a week.

8. Skipping school.

9. Crying and becoming very homesick when staying overnight at a friend's or relative's house.

10. Picking fights with other children.

11. Lying to parents three times a week.

12. Eating such large quantities of junk food that they feel sick to their stomachs three times a month.

13. In looking over the list you just completed, what generalization might you make about children's developmental level and psychopathology?

14. At what age should the *DSM* stop considering age as an integral part of its classification for mental disorders? Why?

15. Can you think of a more efficient method of classifying disorders while allowing for developmental maturation?

16. If Erik Erikson is right and we continue to develop emotionally and socially throughout life, how might his theory impact the classification of mental disorders?

Name _____ Section _____ Date _____

## ACTIVITY 12-4

1. There has been a great deal of discussion and controversy over the inclusion of an overeating disorder in the *DSM*. While many people think it is a serious disorder related to negative social and physical consequences, others say that labeling people who are overweight as mentally disordered will do them much more harm than good. What do you see as the pros and cons of defining an overeating disorder?

2. Develop a diagnostic profile for overeating disorder as it would appear in the next *DSM*. List the criteria needed in order to make such a diagnosis.

3. Critically examine the criteria you developed. Have you made your criteria discrete enough that it will be easy for clinicians to apply only to people with a serious overeating disorder, yet general enough to include those who need to have this diagnosis?

4. Do you believe it may create a pathology for people who might not be mentally disordered?

5. What are the benefits of your new diagnostic criteria?

6. Are there any limitations to your new diagnostic criteria?

7. What was difficult about developing this new diagnostic category?

8. Do you believe this will ever become a valid *DSM* diagnosis? Why or why not?

Name _____ Section _____ Date _____

# ACTIVITY 12-5

Family systems therapy believes that people do not exist in a vacuum. We all are affected by the systems in which we live, work, and play. In attempting to understand and treat clients, family systems therapists attempt to treat the whole system, believing that this is the most effective and efficient way to help people establish better mental health. In many cases it is not realistic to expect the entire family to participate in therapy. However, it is very helpful to get a clear picture of the family system in which clients grew up. Systems therapists would argue that we all continue to play out roles and expectations we assumed when we were growing up. These roles and expectations continue to impact our relationships, sense of selves, and ability to grow.

Two terms used by family systems therapists to describe dysfunctional families are enmeshed and disengaged. Systems therapists have discovered that certain mental disorders are more likely to be associated with enmeshed or disengaged families. People in enmeshed families tend to be overly involved in each other's lives. Family members tend to think for each other. There are no boundaries between individual family members. Many disorders where the issue of control is central—such as anorexia nervosa—develop due to family enmeshment. Alcohol and drug abuse may also be seen as a product of enmeshment.

1. Write a vignette of an enmeshed family that includes a teen daughter who has developed anorexia nervosa.

In the disengaged family, there is little connection or communication between family members. Family members feel little or no support or concern and tend to feel isolated and alienated. Schizoid behavior, promiscuity, and conduct disorders may be related to a disengaged family system.

2. Write a vignette of a disengaged family that has a teen daughter who is promiscuous.

Name _____ Section _____ Date _____

## ACTIVITY 12-6

Parents are the most important influence on children. After reading the chapter on childhood and adolescent disorders, some people question the extent to which parents impact, prevent, or create various childhood disorders.

1. What did your parents do that helped you develop a strong sense of self-esteem, resiliency, and self-efficacy?

2. What did your parents do that may have hurt your development of a stronger sense of self-esteem, resiliency, and self-efficacy?

3. List skills, values, abilities, and attributes that you feel are essential for children to develop in order for them to become high-functioning, happy, well-adjusted adults.

4. List parenting behaviors that you believe are crucial to the development of healthy, well-adjusted children.

5. In examining your lists of parenting behaviors and of skills, values, attributes, and abilities, which might be specific to your culture and might not be necessary or valued in another culture?

6. As you examine these two lists, are there any items that apply more to males than females? If so, why?

# CHAPTER 13

# SEXUAL AND RELATED PROBLEMS OF ADULT LIFE

Amber, a 35-year-old White female, was referred by her medical doctor to Dr. Walleroo, a renowned sex therapist. Amber had gone to her medical doctor because she was "tired of faking it" and was worried that something might be seriously wrong with her because she has never had an orgasm. She has been sexually active since she was 19 years old. Amber is married to a man she says she loves, but who does not know that Amber has never had an orgasm. Amber has said that she can "fake it better than any XXX porno star," but she is tired of faking it and wants to know what a real orgasm feels like. Amber can become aroused and does become lubricated, but she has never experienced anything more than arousal. The medical examination did not reveal anything of a physiological nature that would explain why Amber cannot achieve orgasm.

**PERSONAL HISTORY**

Amber was born in a mid-sized suburban town in Florida. She is the elder of two children; her brother is 2 years younger. Amber's mother died when Amber was 12 years old, and her father remarried when Amber was 18. Amber stated that her young childhood was basically happy. Amber recalled her family as "just an ordinary all-American family" before her mother's illness. Amber's mother was diagnosed with ovarian cancer when Amber was 11. Amber recalled the last year of her mother's life as "a nightmare that I never really woke up from."

Amber grew up in a middle-class family where her father worked as an insurance salesman and her mother stayed home and took care of the family. Amber remembered being a tomboy when she was younger. She enjoyed and excelled at sports. The year before her mother was diagnosed with cancer, her soccer team made it to the state finals. Amber also rode horses and was competing in dressage before her mother got sick. Amber remembered her mother attending every single one of her soccer practices and games. Her father would try to make it to see her big games, but her mother never even missed a practice.

During the year her mother was dying, Amber was forced to give up soccer and sell her horse. Her mother became too ill to take her to practices and games or to drive her to the stables to care for her horse, and Amber's father didn't have the time both to care for Amber's mother and to take on the responsibilities required to keep Amber involved in her sports. Amber was angry and recounted with shame and embarrassment yelling at her parents and crying about having to sell her horse. "I knew I was acting like a spoiled brat, but I was just so sad and scared and felt so powerless that I lashed out."

After a few months, she realized how childishly and selfishly she was acting and apologized to her parents. She said that was a good thing to have done because her mother was able to let go of her guilt and to have a bit more peace. Amber knew her mother was dying and that it was a hard time for both of her parents. Amber said that after her initial temper tantrums and childish selfishness, she was able to be strong for her parents. It was important for her to put on a strong face and never cause her mother any pain. Amber learned to fake being happy and to ignore her own needs.

As Amber recounted this in therapy, she started to laugh. She had an insight. "I guess I was primed at an early age not to feel any needs, and if I did feel any needs to stuff them down. I was rewarded BIG time for never having any needs. I guess this pattern has continued in my sex life."

While Amber was able to "stuff" her needs as an 11-year-old, her 9-year-old brother had many problems. Her brother was kicked out of school for picking fights, picked up by the police for shoplifting, and reported to the police for breaking windows and painting on school walls. Amber said that she believes it was because her brother was scared and angry and refused to stuff his needs and feelings. While he caused her parents a lot of grief, he was able to get some of his needs met a good deal of the time. "I guess it's that squeaky wheel thing—he made the noise and my parents had to pay attention to his needs and to him. I was quiet and got ignored a lot."

Amber had a vivid memory of when her childhood came to an end. One evening about 2 months before her mother died, her father came and sat next to her and told her that pretty soon she would have to be the woman of the house. "He even nicknamed me his 'little missy mom.' He told me he was going to need to count on me to help him out a lot and to help him raise my brother, who was always in trouble. I can remember having these huge mixed emotions. I was proud that my dad needed me and felt he could count on me to help him out. I also remember feeling like the weight of the world had just landed on my poor skinny shoulders. I was 11 years old, for God's sake. What did I know of raising a 9-year-old delinquent, or cooking or cleaning, or being a missy mom?"

Amber recounted that because her mother was so skilled at being a mom, she herself had never learned how to do "mom stuff." Amber's mother did all of the cooking and cleaning. Amber and her brother had never made their own beds, done their own laundry, or even washed the dishes before their mother got sick. After her mother was sick, the house became chaotic. Relatives and friends came over and ran the household, bringing food, cleaning, and doing laundry. On the day her father spoke with Amber, she decided that she would assume all that responsibility, and the next day she began. Amber remembered everyone thinking it was cute that she wanted to take over and that the adults decided to let her do it all because they believed it was her way of handling her mother's dying. Amber remembered a tough couple of months of adjustment while she learned how to do it all, but she did it and never once asked anyone for any help. Amber had another insight as she shared this last point.

> I think I knew there was no one to ask for help. My dad was overwhelmed, and I was supposed to be helping him, and my mom was leaving for good. Who could I ask? What was I supposed to ask? No one in my family ever asked for help. My mom was dying and in great pain and she never once asked for help! I think that's why my dad's telling me I would need to help him by being the "missy mom" made such a huge impression on me. The rules were that we were strong and self-sufficient. I never questioned the rules. Even as an adult, I can't ask for help. Coming for therapy is a huge thing for me.

Amber did not have many friends in junior high or high school. She appeared to be a very serious person and didn't really fit in with the rest of the students. She did have three or four good girlfriends that she grew up with, and they are all still friends today. Amber grew to be an attractive young lady and was popular with boys. She had several steady boyfriends throughout high school. They were never serious or intimate, but were friends who happened to be boys. Amber remained a virgin throughout high school and into college. She fooled around in high school but only to the light petting stage. She was terrified of getting pregnant and wasn't all that interested in sex.

Amber fell in love in the summer between her first and second years of college. Derek was 2 years older than she and was just as serious about life as she. They were both virgins when they met and lost their virginity to each other. Amber recalled it as being very awkward and embarrassing. She said it didn't last very long and that she was surprised when it was over. Amber said that she always enjoyed foreplay and found herself getting excited, but once intercourse started, she would lose her lubrication, and it would begin to hurt. After a few months, Derek became concerned over Amber's lack of lubrication. He asked her on many, many occasions if she had had an orgasm, and Amber always answered that she had. Amber said that in the beginning it wasn't really a total lie because she wasn't sure what was happening. She thought she might have had an orgasm because the foreplay felt so good.

Amber and Derek married a year later. Their marriage was stressful in many ways because they were both focused on building their careers. They decided not to have children, at least right away, so it did not concern either of them when they did not have sex for weeks and weeks. After a year, Amber became concerned over her lack of interest in intercourse. She did some research, watched some pornographic videos, and talked with girlfriends about their sex lives. After this research, Amber decided that something was definitely wrong with her. For the first time in her life, she tried masturbating. At first she became excited and lubricated, and it felt really good. After a while, however, the same thing happened to her as happened when she had sex with Derek—she lost lubrication, and stimulation no longer felt good.

Because Derek had continued to question her about her orgasms, Amber stated that she learned how to fake it well enough that he stopped asking her.

1. Using the following list, make an initial diagnosis for Amber. Discuss your reasons for ruling out or considering specific diagnoses.

    a. Hypoactive sexual desire disorder

    b. Sexual aversion disorder

    c. Female arousal disorder

    d. Female orgasmic disorder

    e. Dyspareunia

    f. Vaginismus

## THERAPY

Amber's physician found no medical reason for Amber's inability to have an orgasm. She recommended that Amber seek counseling in order to treat what appeared to be a psychological problem. Dr. Walleroo uses the "PLISSIT" model of sex therapy. This model is based on the belief that sex therapy needs to progress in stages, from the most basic to the more intense. By following the PLISSIT model, a client addresses his or her initial concerns and proceeds from a basic etiology to the more complex therapy as needed. The steps are as follows:

- *P for permission.* This step involves giving the client explicit permission to be sexual. This is an important step for clients whose problems may be based on a rigid, judgmental upbringing that viewed sex as dirty or wrong.
- *LI for limited information.* During this step, clients are given basic educational facts about anatomy, the sexual response cycle, how other people perform sexually, and how they might expect their bodies to respond.
- *SS for specific suggestions.* This step involves teaching clients the specific techniques to address particular sexual dysfunctions. Sex therapists focus on the problems that prompted the client to seek help.
- *IT for intensive therapy.* This step is one that the majority of clients never need to explore. It is the step that addresses ambivalence and resistance to sex. This step might need to address issues of childhood sexual abuse or molestation, power imbalances within the relationship, or fears concerning sexual orientation.

Dr. Walleroo suggested that Amber learn to relax and enjoy her body (the permission stage). The doctor recommended that Amber start by finding a time when she knew she would be alone and then running a bubble bath for herself. She was then to take a sensual bath by putting a fragrance that she found soothing in the water, lighting some candles in the bathroom, dimming the lights, putting on some favorite relaxing music, turning off the phone, and taking a bath. While in the bath, Amber was to feel her body, running her hands around her body and exploring the texture of her skin and the contours of her shape. She was not to try to sexually stimulate herself, but just to explore and enjoy her body. Amber reported that she enjoyed this homework assignment. She was concerned, though, because she did not become sexually aroused by it. Dr. Walleroo assured her that this was exactly right—all she was doing now was getting to know her body better.

After talking some more about her history, Dr. Walleroo gave Amber another homework assignment. She was to go home and find another safe time. During this time she was to find a full-length mirror, dim the lights, light some candles, put on some favorite music, and do a striptease in front of the mirror. After she had removed all of her clothes, she was to look at her body. She was to uncritically explore the contours and contrasts of her body, enjoying all the various shapes and textures.

At the next session, Amber reported that the experience was interesting. She said that she had never really looked at her body like that before. When she first started the striptease, she was embarrassed and self-conscious, but that once she got going she liked it. "After I was naked I was beginning to get really critical—you know, look at that dimple or roll, etc. But then I realized I was really rather beautiful, not in a Playboy way, but in a real way. I was always fairly happy with my body before because it was solid and functional and required little maintenance, kind of like a Honda! I never had to diet or do a lot of exercising to stay in shape, and I am never sick, so my body is functional. But as I stood there I realized that while it might be a Honda, it could be seen by some to be a luxury model, kind of sleek and curved in the right places!"

Amber and Dr. Walleroo talked about the need to tell Derek that Amber was not having orgasms. Amber feared that telling Derek this would hurt his feelings. They agreed that Amber would think about the necessity of being honest with Derek and allowing him to become involved in her therapy.

At this point, Dr. Walleroo went over some basic human sexuality information with Amber. The doctor discussed basic anatomy, talked about the differences many women felt with vaginal versus clitoral stimulation, and reviewed the sexual response cycle. Amber was given the homework assignment to take another sensual bath and intentionally explore her genitals and breasts and allow herself to become excited, with no pressure to orgasm. As soon as it stopped feeling good, Amber could stop.

Amber reported back that she had again enjoyed her homework assignment, and that she did not orgasm although she did enjoy the stimulation for a long while. "I was able to really enjoy the process without any pressure. I think that when I am having intercourse or masturbating I focus so much on the 'Big O' that I lose the enjoyment of the moment. I also think that I know I'm going to fail, so I do." Amber also told Dr. Walleroo that after thinking about it, she had decided that it was the right thing to tell Derek. She asked if she could bring Derek to her next session and tell him during the session. Dr. Walleroo agreed. Amber's homework was to continue to explore her body and to find the ways that she liked to be touched.

Derek came to the next session. He was very worried about what was happening because Amber would only tell him that she was in therapy and needed him to be involved. Dr. Walleroo asked Amber if she felt comfortable telling Derek what this was all about. Amber said she'd try, and then she began to cry. Derek became very concerned and scared; he thought Amber was going to say that she was dying or wanted a divorce. After the doctor helped Amber to calm down, she told Derek that she was unhappy because she wasn't able to have an orgasm, that she was ashamed for faking it and lying to him, and that she loved him and hoped he would understand. Derek immediately went to Amber and held her and told her he loved her. After she had calmed down, Derek also told Amber that she deserved an Academy Award.

Derek was very concerned that he wasn't doing things right so that Amber could have an orgasm. Dr. Walleroo explained that Amber had never had an orgasm, and that there were things that Amber and Derek could do together that might help. Dr. Walleroo assigned some exercises, called sensate focus, designed by Masters and Johnson. Amber and Derek had to agree to try these exercises with the understanding that they were not to lead to intercourse. Derek and Amber were to find things that felt good, like feathers, satin, and velvet. Then they were to find a time and place they could feel safe and relax together, get naked, and just touch each other. First one person would be the receiver of the touch for 30 minutes, and then they would switch. The receiver would not be allowed to touch back until the time was up; all he or she could do would be to say what felt good and to receive the touch. During the week, Amber was to continue to explore masturbation.

The next session Amber and Derek reported their homework sessions to be a huge success. They both enjoyed the exercise very much, though they found it difficult not to reciprocate the touching or to stop touching before it led to intercourse. Amber reported enjoying her exploration of masturbation and wanted to try using a vibrator. Dr. Walleroo agreed. He assigned another exercise for Amber and Derek to try. In this exercise, one partner lies down with the partner lying alongside. The partner who is to receive first places his or her hands lightly on top of the partner's hands and guides the partner's hands to the places that feel good. He or she also guides the partner's hands in the rhythm, motion, and strength of touch he or she likes.

The next session Amber and Derek came in beaming and laughing. Amber said that she tried a wand vibrator while masturbating and had her first orgasm. She was so excited that she felt safe enough to demonstrate for Derek that night. They did the homework assignment, but confessed that they broke the rules and had intercourse. They were both smiling and laughing as they confessed this to Dr. Walleroo. They then told Dr. Walleroo that Amber had her first orgasm during intercourse as well.

Dr. Walleroo asked them to do the exercise again and to have intercourse only once that week. They were to plan a romantic and sensual evening together later this week. There was to be no pressure for Amber to have an orgasm during intercourse, but to just enjoy the intimacy. Amber was to continue to explore masturbation with and without the vibrator.

The following week, Amber and Derek reported that the exercise was a success. They both had enjoyed the exercise and the intercourse. Although Amber did not have an orgasm during intercourse, she was able to have an orgasm after intercourse through oral stimulation, and she continued to orgasm during masturbation.

Dr. Walleroo did not feel it was necessary to continue on to the level of intensive therapy. Amber's problem was resolved. Dr. Walleroo discharged Amber.

1. Do you think Dr. Walleroo made the right decision to discharge Amber? Why or why not?

2. Do you think Amber will ever need to resolve any of her childhood issues? Why or why not?

3. What do you see as the strengths and weaknesses of PLISSIT sex therapy?

Name _____ Section _____ Date _____

## ACTIVITY 13-1

**Vignette 1**

Sydney is a 27-year-old White flight attendant who has been suspended from his job because female passengers filed numerous complaints against him. Sydney has been accused of rubbing up against female passengers in an inappropriate manner. Sydney claims that he is just trying to do his job and that because the aisles are so narrow he must sometimes lean into a passenger to allow someone else to get past him or to put something up into an overhead compartment. The female passengers who complained stated that Sydney would rub up against their shoulders if they were seated or against their thighs or buttocks if they were standing, and that many times they could not see any valid reason for Sydney to lean into them or to rub against them. The female passengers stated that they could feel that Sydney was sexually aroused.

1. What *DSM-IV* diagnosis would you assign to Sydney?

2. Do you think what Sydney was doing should be considered a sex crime? Why or why not?

**Vignette 2**

Janice is a 47-year-old female who came for counseling after her doctor could find no medical reason for Janice's problems. Janice states that she looks forward to having sex and that she can get lubricated and excited. She reaches orgasm through masturbation, but every time she tries to have intercourse with her new husband "something happens down there and I seem to close up." Janice will become lubricated and can enjoy manual penetration of her vagina, but as soon as she anticipates penile penetration her muscles tense up and will not allow penetration. This muscle tension causes her a great deal of pain if her husband attempts to force his penis into her vagina. Janice states that this is a new phenomenon. She and her husband had been able to enjoy intercourse before marriage.

3. What *DSM-IV* diagnosis would you assign to Janice?

4. What sort of psychological dynamics might be affecting Janice?

**Vignette 3**

Michael is a 25-year-old male who loves to dress up in women's clothes. His favorite movie is *Priscilla, Queen of the Desert;* he can relate to the characters and would love to be a professional female impersonator. Michael has been a homosexual for as long as he can remember. He never had any sexual interest in girls, but loved to wear their clothes, saying that they are beautiful and feel good. He performs as a female impersonator at an amateur club on weekends. He states that he enjoys wearing men's clothes, too. He has never wanted to be a woman; he just likes to perform as a woman. When he has sex with someone he does not dress up.

5. What *DSM-IV* diagnosis would you assign to Michael? Why?

**Vignette 4**

Alex is a 34-year-old male who is very depressed and anxious. He states that his life is falling apart because he can't seem to control his sexual urges. He spends a great deal of his time thinking about sex, fantasizing about sex, and seeking out sexual partners. He says that his marriage is on the rocks because he can't seem to stop having affairs. He loves his wife and adores his two daughters, but the thrill of sexual conquest is overpowering at times. His job is in jeopardy because he made an inappropriate pass at his female boss. Alex admits to engaging in unprotected sex at times and is terrified that he might become infected with hepatitis or AIDS.

6. Using the *DSM-IV* criteria for a mental disorder, do you think that Alex meets the criteria? Why or why not?

7. Do you think that sex addiction should be considered a *DSM* diagnosis? What are the pros and cons of including it as a diagnosis?

Name _____ Section _____ Date _____

## ACTIVITY 13-2

Imagine that an alien from Mars has come to your college as an exchange student. It is your responsibility to explain sexual norms in America to this student. Do a thorough job of explaining our norms.

1. What is sex?

2. What is considered normal, acceptable sexual behavior for:

   a. Children under 12 years old

   b. Teens from the ages of 12 to 18

   c. Young adults who are not married

CHAPTER 13 / SEXUAL AND RELATED PROBLEMS OF ADULT LIFE   213

d. Young adults who are married

e. Middle-aged adults who are single

f. Middle-aged adults who are married

g. Older adults who are single

h. Older adults who are married

i. Gay or lesbian teenagers

j. Gay or lesbian adults

3. How do people in our society learn the rules governing appropriate sexual behavior?

4. What happens to people in our society who deviate from the norms?

5. How does change happen within our society?

Name _____ Section _____ Date _____

## ACTIVITY 13-3

1. The vast majority of people with paraphilias—well over 95 percent—are men. List the reasons you think this discrepancy might exist.

2. Review your list. As you looked at your answers, did you find any biases or stereotypes? Where do you think your beliefs may have come from? What were some of your belief patterns?

Listed below are some alternative explanations. Critically think about each explanation and write some arguments for and against each. (Use additional sheets of paper as needed.)

3. The male hormone (testosterone) is much more powerful than the female hormone (estrogen). As a result, men's sexual desires and needs are much stronger than women's. This unequal sex drive causes men to develop more sexual deviancy than women.

4. Men's gender identity is much more repressed than women's. Women are allowed much more freedom in their ability to express themselves in the way they dress, play, and relate to other people. Look at the differences between the treatment of a boy who enjoys wearing dresses, playing with dolls, and expressing emotions and a girl who enjoys wearing jeans, playing with toy cars, and not expressing a lot of emotions. This repression of gender identity development can cause men to develop deviant sexual desires.

5. Women actually have many deviant sexual desires and habits, but society does not condemn women for acting on them. For example, a woman who has exhibitionist desires can become a stripper or a topless waitress and get paid for her exhibitionism. A man becomes a flasher and is labeled deviant.

6. Women's sexuality in our society is still very repressed. Women probably do have many deviant desires, but because they are not supposed to have sexual needs or desires, women continue to repress any strong sexual desire, normal or deviant.

7. The XY combination in males is weaker than the XX combination in females. Because of the inherent fragility of the XY pairing, men are at greater risk for aberrations of a sexual nature. The XX combination protects women from developing sexual aberrations.

8. Society shapes and conditions men to view everything as sexual. As a result, men are at higher risk for developing deviant sexual desires. Women are not conditioned to view as many things as sexual, so they develop fewer deviant sexual desires.